HOW TO ANALYZE PEOPLE 2-IN-1 BUNDLE

NLP 2.0 Mastery + Dark Psychology - The #1 Ultimate Box Set to Proven Manipulation Techniques and Influence People Effortlessly

NLP 2.0 MASTERY - HOW TO ANALYZE PEOPLE

Discover How to Read and Influence People with Proven Body Language and Persuasion Methods, Even if You are a Clueless Beginner

© Copyright 2018 - All rights reserved.

The following book is reproduced below with the goal of providing information that is as accurate and reliable as possible. Regardless, purchasing this book can be seen as consent to the fact that both the publisher and the author of this book are in no way experts on the topics discussed within and that any recommendations or suggestions that are made herein are for entertainment purposes only. Professionals should be consulted as needed prior to undertaking any of the action endorsed herein.

This declaration is deemed fair and valid by both the American Bar Association and the Committee of Publishers Association and is legally binding throughout the United States.

Furthermore, the transmission, duplication, or reproduction of any of the following work including specific information will be considered an illegal act irrespective of if it is done electronically or in print. This extends to creating a secondary or tertiary copy of the work or a recorded copy and is only allowed with the express written consent from the Publisher. All additional right reserved.

The information in the following pages is broadly considered a truthful and accurate account of facts and as such, any inattention, use, or misuse of the information in question by the reader will render any resulting actions solely under their purview. There are no scenarios in which the publisher or the original author of this work can be in any fashion deemed liable for any hardship or damages that may befall them after undertaking information described herein.

Additionally, the information in the following pages is intended only for informational purposes and should thus be thought of as universal. As befitting its nature, it is presented without assurance regarding its prolonged validity or interim quality. Trademarks that are mentioned are done without written consent and can in no way be considered an endorsement from the trademark holder.

Table of Contents

Introduction 7
Introduction to NLP 8
    The Subconscious Mind 16
    Secret Driving Habits 20
Development and Learning 26
    Perspective 32
Take Charge of Your Mind 36
    Your Inner Voice 42
    Dropping Anchors 45
    Dissociation 48
    Content Reframing 49
The Art of Persuasion and Manipulation 51
    Habitual Thinking 53
    Meta-Programs of NLP 54
    Internal Representation 57
    Communication Model 60
    Three Components of NLP 64
Analyzing Body Language and the Mind 66
    Understanding Body Language 67
    Meta Model 71
    The Right Questions 74
    Personal Beliefs 79
Building Connections 81
    Building Rapport 82
    Using Your Words and Voice 89
    Conflict Resolution 93
NLP Applications 97
Conclusion 99

Congratulations on downloading *NLP: The Ultimate Guide to Manipulation* and thank you for doing so.

This book is meant to be an introduction and guide to NLP or Neuro-Linguistic Programming. Basically, NLP is the science and art of excellence, which was created from looking at how the top people in various careers were able to obtain their results. The communication skills herein can be learned by everyone to help their effectiveness both professionally and personally

Thanks again for choosing this book! Every effort was made to ensure it is full of as much useful information as possible. Please enjoy!

Introduction

You will find many NLP models that will help you in every aspect of your life and career. The approach you will find is practical, you will see results and it is growing in influence in many different disciplines.

Since NLP is constantly growing and evolving and this book is static, it will work as a snapshot of NLP. Even though things may be different tomorrow, it doesn't mean that the practice in this book won't be helpful.

You should view this information as a stepping stone. It is giving you a chance to explore a new area and to keep your life exciting. This book is meant for the beginner to easily understand what to do without confusion.

NLP is a state of mind and a way of being. NLP is something practical that has to be done. While reading about it will teach you a lot, you have to actively practice it to reap any benefits. You will find sets of models, techniques, and skills that will change the way you act and think. This is meant to be useful and to improve your life.

You have to find out what works by doing it. Then you can figure out what didn't work and then work with that until you are able to make it work. This is the great thing about NLP. Let's get started.

There are plenty of books on this subject on the market, so thanks again for choosing this one! Every effort was made to ensure it is full of as much useful information as possible. Please enjoy!

Introduction to NLP

A person's behavior is based on specific structures. With NLP or Neuro-Linguistic Programming, the way that people act, speak, and think is examine with models. Richard Bandler has patterned these models. In the beginning, he patterned his work after characters like Virginia Stair, Fritz Perls, and Milton Erickson, who were seen to have amazing behavioral and linguistic abilities.

Your own experiences are the main uses of the NLP system. There is no way to learn NLP through sequential steps and techniques. However, programmers become skilled at using methods to change how the brain functions and perceives. Its goal is to create a good foundation of attitude and skill so that they can produce new techniques and approaches to self-preserve.

You aren't going to only depend on steps and techniques that are taught to you. You are going to learn how to create new steps so that you can continually achieve success. It works as an investigation of knowledge that will use different stage of human attitude and development, as well as thought formation.

It is going to give you effective tools and strategies that will define who you are, the role you play, and your ideal state of success. While the initial state begins with you, the process will involve all of those around you and the environment to create the best mindset.

The purpose behind NLP is to work as a toolbox of thoughts, skills, and attitudes. The models will become patterns through which your habits will change and be redefined. When you plan on using NLP, you are aiming for personal development and success.

NLP can also make you successful. Whether you are faced with problems in your family, work, or leisure, NLP will give you the ability to alter your outlook and view towards the world. You will start to notice the important meaning of life and what priorities are important in your life. Once you are able to find your strong and weak areas, you will be able to focus on what will make you successful and efficient.

NLP will also improve communication. Positive thinking is able to be changed into words. You will end up becoming more verbally competent when you learn how to change your thoughts and emotions and the way you share perspectives and how you communicate with others. Communication is an amazing method that will give you a better influence, a larger network of friends, and a better way to express yourself.

NLP will also bring together the mind, body, and emotions. There are a lot of people who experience difficulty putting all of the plans into actionable steps. Other people aren't able to learn from their experiences. When these things happen, it means that your mind, body, and emotions aren't working together. Through the use of NLP, you will be able to make connections with each aspect of your existence. NLP will allow all of these aspects to work together so that you can reach success.

To help explain NLP, let's take a look at the history. NLP was first created in the '70s by Richard Bandler and John Grinder. This development was created at the University of California and supervised by Gregory Bateson. Bandler, Bateson, and Grinder were influenced by Alfred Korzybski because of his theories surrounding human presuppositions and modeling.

Other contributors to the theory were Leslie Cameron-Bandler, David Gordon, Judith DeLozier, and Robert Dilts.

Grinder and Bandler worked on the NLP theory until they had a falling out in the '80s. Ginder and DeLozier later created the New Code which took a mind and body approach. Bandler's approach looked at Ericksonian submodalities and hypnosis. Michael Hall mainly looked at mental states and neuro-semantics.

Ted James looked at the best periods of life for therapy and Anthony Robbins made use of products that use NLP. At this point, NLP had been managed and created in different independent sectors. It had also grown and been renamed several times over. Then again, it has also suffered from a lack of definition and regulation.

After many different legal battles, legally, NLP has now become a generic term. Even after all of these years, NLP practitioners still don't have an agreement in regard to the theory. That's why a lot of people have abused it. Still, a lot of the work is dependent on the ideas of the co-developers and other such individuals. For a person to formally practice NLP for human development and condition, they will need to become certified.

Why is it called Neuro-Linguistic Programming? "Neuro" refers to the brain, which what controls your behavior and actions and it stores your memories and experiences. "Linguistic" comes from the word language. This means the "neuro-linguistic" refers to how language affects the brain. Non-verbal cues, words, and symbols are able to cause a response. "Programming" is used to describe the mechanism that is analogous to a computer program.

There are presuppositions of Neuro-Linguistic Programming. The NLP foundation comes with a few basic presuppositions.

Every technique, model, and strategy that is connected to NLP is used along with these assumptions. Since NLP studies the subjective experience, an assumption would be that people can determine objective reality.

The perfect or best direction for life is non-existent. This is the reason why a person can only reach the best possible moment and hope that they have the correct attitude to make the best choices. A person's objective in using NLP is to find excellence and wisdom. Once you widen your choices, you will also be improving your odds of finding excellence. When you are able to acquire different views of the environment, you will gain wisdom.

A territory and a map are not the same things. You can't live your life with only one direct route. Humans are given several different options on the ways that they can live their lives. Depending on what your experiences and perceptions are, you will make decisions that you take you on different paths.

You are in possession of a map to your reality, which will involve a representation of you and those around you. With this map, you will be able to react to the world and be able to better understand yourself. However, if you end up having too much discrepancy between your personal map and territory, you could end up getting lost.

Your life and mind work in systematic processes. There is always going to be an interaction between two people or between a person and the environment. Everything within the universe is connected to each other. When something in your mind or life is affected, your whole experience will absorb what happens. This connection is needed to keep a constant balance.

Communication elicits a response and it comes with a meaning. The manner and content of the reply you receive from the person you are communicating with is the point of your communication. Even if you are aiming to deliver a certain message, validation of understanding can only happen when one person has responded properly.

For example, if you are telling a joke and the person you were telling it to didn't laugh or understand it, then the manner of your telling of the joke didn't help your expected response.

There are two levels of communication — conscious and unconscious. Verbal communication is only one form of communication. A lot of people aren't aware of the fact that they use a lot of body language, facial expressions, posturing, hand and eye movements, and non-verbal cues while they are talking. People are even able to add to the tone and mood of the conversation to relay the message more effectively. Take the statement, "Get out of here." This statement can be communicated in several different ways that could relay a positive or negative message.

Communication can't fail, it only gets an outcome. A person can't say that their communication was useless or was a failure if they didn't get the response they wanted. All it means is that the result ended up being different than what they had expected. This should influence the person to enhance their skills and attitude in regards to communication. You must learn from unpleasant outcomes so that you can identify and gauge the things that kept you from sending out the correct message.

Rapport, which we talk in depth about later on, relates to people according to their world. Each person is able to make their own model or representation of the world that are based on their understanding of environmental influences and previous experiences. This is the reason why you will need to exert some effort if you want to create a new model.

It's important that you are able to see the world as others do so that you can build rapport and communicate effectively. If you keep your mind close in regards to their representation, you will likely have a very hard time getting the response you are looking for. Other people could have a hard time understanding your model.

If a communicator is inflexible, it will be seen through their resistance. When you find that the person you are talking with is resistant, this doesn't mean that they are closed off to the communication. It could mean that you have established rapport. Thus, you will need to enter into their world model. Otherwise, they won't be able to unconsciously receive your message. You also need to learn how you can become flexible so that you are able to understand and speak their language. This is especially true because they can't understand yours. You could end up insulting them without knowing it if you aren't flexible.

You don't have to obtain new things just so that you can be a good leader or communicator. You don't have to obtain new things to create positive changes. You have everything that you already need. All of the mental, emotional, and behavioral resources are within you.

If you aren't able to see them, then you haven't created an access to them. You are not aware of your strengths. You could have a lot of chronic stressors that will keep you from using them. Through NLP, you will be able to be more aware of the resources you have and learn how to correctly use them.

Your positive worth will stay the same even if your internal and external behavior is in question. All humans have worth and dignity no matter what their thoughts and actions are. Then there are good and bad behaviors that will determine their judgment of worth to themselves and the environment.

Your value won't change no matter how bad you act. The value of your actions and behavior are measured based on the expectations of those around you. You are able to change your bad actions and manners so that you can come into alignment with your values.

Every behavior is meant to have a good outcome. However, not every behavior is supposed to be done with positive manners. There are self-preserving mechanisms that are meant for personal benefits. The process of this goal can be dangerous for you and others. These types of behaviors could be unconscious. Your mind and body have a tendency to think about a positive outcome and end up neglecting negative manners.

You have to make sure that you don't rush into decisions or actions without getting the information that you need. You also need to make sure that you take the time to calm down. Disrupted emotions and haste will often cause inadequacy in your actions and bad judgment. You have to be able to differentiate automated and conscious responses. You also need to be able to see the difference between ideals and realities. You should give yourself a reality check every now and again so that you can up your odds of making the best decision.

The process of NLP assimilates subjective experiences. Ever since the moment you started to remember your life events, your brain has worked tirelessly to store information. This information is then recalled through memories and experiences that are changed into personal beliefs and perceptions. These beliefs could be negative or positive depending on how you react to your previous experiences. Positive beliefs can be kept and negative ones can be replaced by positive ones.

NLP works by changing your false or negative understandings.

When you are able to connect your brain to your senses, you will find that you can let go of negative feelings, vague thoughts, and traumatic experiences. You have the power to get rid of whatever is hindering you from living a successful and happy life.

For NLP to be effective, every part needs to work together. The first part is the neurological aspect. Your nervous system will take in your experiences using the five senses — smell, taste, touch, hearing, and sight. Your nervous system will then send out signals to the brain so that you can make sense of them.

Then you have the language aspect. This includes verbal and non-verbal communication. These systems of communication order and code your neural representations to provide them meaning. The last part is programming. This is your brain's ability to organize the information from each system. The organization is the way that you achieve specific results and goals. When all three systems are used in unison, you will get a synergistic effect. This allows you to get your desired results.

NLP will help you to perform several different functions. As I have said, it will help your communication skills. NLP can be used to create behavioral changes in others and ourselves. It will provide you with different perspectives of the outside world. These new perspectives will help you to adjust your behaviors and attitudes.

Through NLP, you will become more aware of the things you do. Most people don't pay attention to their actions and thoughts. NLP provides you with a process that will keep you grounded and in control.

Everybody sees the world through different filters. These filters will use different beliefs and values. NLP can help you get rid of these filters. This will give you a better view of the other person's point of view. It will also give you the ability to understand how your actions will affect the lives of others.

NLP is able to create a real difference. You will find improved information. You are able to use this improved information to make the best decisions. The better decisions will bring you better actions. Better actions will give you better results.

The Subconscious Mind

Do you remember the song, "Should I Stay or Should I Go?" This is a great example of something that everything will experience from time to time. It's that inner conflict that makes it feel like one part of us want to do one thing, and then another part is interested in doing something else. Or it could manifest when we feel uncertain about what we actually want to do.

Trying to create change in yourself is easy when everything is congruent, meaning that you are in harmony with yourself and completely dedicated to making the change. You end up being incongruent when you go through an internal conflict which doesn't facilitate your change process. Internal conflict will come up when you split yourself between wanting to do two different things at one time but you can't do both at the same time. For example, when somebody asks you to do a favor, you are torn between wanting to help them and continue doing what you are currently doing. This is when your tone of voice and body language changes. You may tell them — yes, but your body signs won't show the same enthusiasm.

Another example would be when you feel uncertain between two conflicting choices. A part of you is going to want to do something while the other part has a different idea. At that moment, you want to do both of those things.

Incongruence can also be noticed in pleasant conflicts such as part of you wants to go to the beach and another part wants to go to the mountains. The important thing is when incongruence causes a conflict with your values. Let's take this as an example, your boss told you that you need to show a certain customer more aggression. To you, being aggressive means that you are being pushy and pushiness goes against your values.

There will be times when you find yourself associated with incongruent people who will cause you to feel unsure of yourself as to the best way to handle them. They could agree to go along with you or do something, but their face tells you a different story. Other types of incongruent people will tell you that they will do something for you, but they end up changing their mind.

You have probably had times where you didn't have a doubt in your mind and everything was going smoothly. A lot of people call this as "being in the zone." This is how you know you are congruent. Figuring out when you are and when you aren't congruent is a very good life skill. The more aware you are of your own signals of incongruence, the quicker you will be at resolving the conflict. The faster you are able to resolve your incongruence, the easier things will become since you won't be spinning your wheels and unconsciously debating or resisting something.

Incongruence causes a lot of friction in your life. It will take a lot of energy to overcome that part of you that wants to do something that opposes a course of action. The more you work at overriding that part, the more likely it will become that the other part of you is going to object. And when you are faced with fighting with yourself, you normally always lose.

It's a lot easier and more effective to develop the ability to notice when you are incongruent and fix it. It is one of the easier skills to develop and it gives you the most reward. The biggest source of physical and emotional stress is when your mind is trying extremely hard to override the big desire of your body to keep you from doing something that will violate your values. The best way to live a fulfilling life is to move in harmony with your values.

- Recognizing Incongruence

You have probably had several recent moments of being congruent about something. Take a moment to think of the first one of those recent moments that you can think of. Now, take a moment to very specifically remember the place and time where you had that feeling. Remember what you felt, what you heard, and what and who you saw. Remember that moment as if you were living right now. What is it that you are seeing? What things are you hearing? What do you feel?

Recalling that moment is pretty empowering, right? Now pick an aspect of that moment, whether it is a picture, something you felt, or something you heard. The aspect needs to be what is most important to you. This is all in your mind, so whichever element seems the most important to you at that moment.

Now, place that to the side and think about the opposite. Think of a moment when you were uncertain. A moment where you felt extremely ambivalent about something that you needed to do. You will likely find that it's easier to come up with an example when you think about the last time a person asked you to do something and you didn't want to.

Take that feeling, image, or sound you have and magnify it.

Make it grow larger, louder, stronger, or brighter. You want to make sure that you are able to recognize it each time it happens. This will be your warning. This is what will let you know that you have to pay attention and sort what all is happening. When you receive that signal, you need to stop, take a step back, and assess what is going on.

If you make this congruence check a habit when you are looking at your dreams and goals, you will become less likely to find yourself in situations where you are in conflict with others and yourself.

Understanding the incongruence that other people may have will make it easier for you to accept this as a normal thing. You only have to seek out clarification of their incongruence by asking them for a reason behind their less than enthusiastic look when they provide you with a positive reply. You should want to understand why they are incongruent as there could be something else that will need to be handled.

We won't all be congruent with every single person that we come in contact with. The way we act when we are with our female friends is going to be different than how you act around your male friends. The way we act around our parents, doctor, teachers or even a cop who pulls us over is going to all be different.

We are all made up of different parts and those parts will be used for every situation that we find ourselves in when we meet a person. When every working part is connected into a whole, we are working congruently.

- Disassociated or Associated

Remember the memories that you recalled for the congruence checklist? You likely have noticed that you were emotionally impacted in different ways in both situations. In the first memory, you were "in" what happened. In NLP, this is known as an associated experience. In your second memory, you were "outside" of the memory and observing what happened. This is what is known as a disassociated experience.

Using the technique of disassociation and association is extremely useful. When you are associated with an image or a memory, no matter if it's imaginary or real, it will be a lot more intense. When you are disassociated from a memory, you watch yourself in it, like a movie. You get information from that moment, but you won't experience an emotional impact.

When you can recall an experience in a disassociated way, you will be able to be an impartial judge. Think back to your two memories. The first you were associated and felt everything. In the second, you were disassociated and observed everything from the outside. Everything was "over there." If there is a memory that makes you feel yucky, then you should always visit it disassociated. There is no reason to feel all of those bad feelings again. You can get information out of it by viewing it as a movie. There are a lot of powerful ways to deal with really traumatic memories.

Secret Driving Habits

Your driving habits are the moments that take you from point A to point B. Most likely, these are strategies that you have created over the years, unconsciously. The ability to change up the process that you experience your reality tends to be more valuable than actually changing the content of your experience of reality.

A strategy is a sequence of steps that you take to perform a certain task. These are your driving habits. It's important to know that a strategy is not the same thing as a behavior. Strategies are unconscious, therefore they become a decision-making process that happened before you were even aware of the external stimulus. In fact, that moment of awareness will typically coincide with the strategies output.

For example, if you don't like spiders, then your strategy has been completed long before you are even aware that a spider is in the room. Your strategy is the decision process you go through, and when you model talented people, it is the decision they make that you have to value.

Pretty much anybody is able to mimic a behavior. The main thing that marks the difference between average and exemplary performance is being able to make decisions that help create that behavior.

Driving a car is made up of a simple behavior set. Your hands and your feet move up and down but knowing when you should do this and how much, is what makes you able to drive. When you started driving, all you did was go through the motions. You didn't make any decisions about where you were going, how fast you wanted to get there, when you stopped or started, and when you turned. The only thing you could manage to do was operate the car. Everything else was above your competency. As you became accustomed to the mechanical movements, you were able to relax and concentrate on the world around you. You soon realized that there were other cars and people out there and that the road could be a dangerous place. You have to learn how to navigate the different obstacles. Most of the learning process is mental and not mechanical. We aren't able to see a person do the mental part, though. We have to assume that playing football, driving a car, or practicing Tai Chi are all physical skills. They are actually physical movements that were manifested from a complex mental process.

Your strategies, then, are a habitual decision that will result in a course of action based upon a specific stimulus. If you were to come up with a skill for goal setting, it could be made up of:

1. A visual view of what you want.
2. A bodily check for congruence with the outcome.
3. A visual recall of the current situation.
4. A visual view of the steps that need to be taken for the outcome.
5. A bodily check for congruence with the outcome.

Basically, a person will imagine what they want to have, they feel good about it, they imagine what they have to do to reach it, and if it still feels good, they act upon it.

The TOTE model was created in 1960 as an extension to the Stimulus-Response that was created by researchers like Pavlov. Basically, what it means is that you have an unconscious way of knowing that you should start something, a way of knowing to continue it, and a way to know when to stop, and then you can stop thinking.

The TOTE model will provide another layer of formality to your basic strategy because it gives you criteria for beginning and ending your strategy. TOTE means Test Operate Test Exit. TOTE is basically the start and stop points for your strategy. You understand that you should shake hands with a person you have met and you see they have their hand outstretched, and you understand that you should stop when the handshake is finished. You can easily see different strategies working when that other person holds your hand for a bit longer or your hands don't make a good connection. You may even have an experience where you shook hands with a person who didn't intend on shaking your hand.

To make things easier when it comes to writing down a strategy, you can use the following notation:

- V – Visual
- At – Auditory Tonal
- Ad – Auditory Digital (language)
- K – Kinesthetic
- O – Olfactory (smell)
- G – Gustatory (taste)
- I – Internal
- E – External
- C – Constructed
- R – Recalled

VI indicates that there is a mental image that could be recalled like a picture of a recent night out or it could be constructed like a picture of you on a night out in the future. External stimuli happen in real time and can't be recalled or constructed. This provides you with an important distinction when it comes to understanding meta-programs. This is specific to the idea that every meta-program has context specific results of external or internal focus of attention. Here is an example of a strategy using the notation from above:

Oe > OiR > ViC > Ki

This shows that the person smelled something in the outside world that made them remember smelling something. Then they internally visualize and experience and then experience a feeling about this and create a conclusion or a judgment.

A strategies exit or conclusion is most often an internal notion. You will often hear people describe this moment when they say something feels right, or they experience a gut feeling, or they just knew that it was going to go wrong or right. All of these feelings are a result of the activation of glands and muscles.

For example, you could see something while you're shopping and remember one that you have at home. You then say to yourself, "I could use a new one" and then you experience a desire to buy it. This same structure could apply to you seeing an apple and then comparing it to an internal apple representation. You then say to yourself, "This is a nice looking apple." This makes you want to eat it.

Strategies, for everybody, tend to be consistent in several different contexts. After all, why should we waste our time learning a new strategy? Life is basically very conservative and as humans, we like to stay consistent, so to elicit a strategy is one context that tends to be valuable for different contexts. The only way to test a strategy is through consistency. If a person is able to get the same result without the need to think about something, the strategy is working perfectly and their behavior is working correctly because they are getting what they want. Keep in mind, each behavior is started with a positive intention and is meant to achieve something. Whether it ends up being good or bad will all depend on the context.

There is a problem when we represent behavioral decisions this way. How are you supposed to know if this is indeed a person that you need to shake hands with? Do you know this person? Is this a social thing? Has anybody else shaken their hand? Is your hand sticky? Do you have a glass in your hand? Are they interested in meeting you? Once you have started to shake hands, how many times should you shake it? How long should you hold it? When do you need to release their hand? How do you let their hand go?

Even a simple thing as shaking a hand can be broken down into several different decision points that would be very hard to represent in a TOTE flowchart. In order to understand your behavior for a certain strategy, you have to assume a lot of things.

Development and Learning

One great way to understand how people are able to learn is to understand how the brain and mental abilities are created. Scientists, through experimentation, can deduce how children are able to see the world in a different way than many adults. This way we are able to see the stages of learning from various angles.

Children tend to take a long time to reach full mental maturity. As a species, humans are unusual in that human babies can't fend for themselves right after they are born. Several other mammals are able to walk and stand within minutes of being born, but since a human has a large head, a baby has a brain that hasn't fully developed.

Our mental capacity also comes at a cost. We have an extended development time once we are born. This is when we are extremely vulnerable and have to be protected by our parents. There must be several months of learning before the baby is able to do things that a calf or lamb can do right after they are born.

Psychologists are able to use this extended developmental period to study the way children learn, how they view the world, the way they think, and how they develop. Jean Piaget, a Swiss scientist, conducted large amounts of research and came up with several developmental stages that child will most likely progress through, and this created the basis of a lot of child psychology and developmental testing.

Children live in a sensory world. Play a game of "peek-a-boo" with a baby and you will notice that the baby is delighted and surprised every time they see your face. How come the baby is surprised over and over again? Surely, they should know that the face is still there but was hidden from their sight. In fact, a baby's worldly experience is so concrete and built upon their sense, when they can't see something, to them, it no longer exists.

As they age, they will explore and start to create "maps" of their surroundings. There will come an age when a child isn't surprised by your reappearing face and you will notice a different behavior. When you hide your face or a toy, the child will start to try to find it.

The child has a conflict in data. They think the toy doesn't exist anymore, but past experience tells them that the toy is only out of sight. The child will then try to resolve this problem. Between the ages of four and 12 months, the child will begin to use their internal map and they will value their own internal data with the external data.

Several years later, while at a magic show, that delight and surprise will be rekindled when a child tries to find the ball in the magician's hand, but it turns out to be empty. The more you allow the child to be exposed to sensory experiences, the more information they will have to create maps and create new ways to view their world.

Let's quickly go over the developmental phases of a child:

- Sensorimotor: zero to two years

This is during the time the child is developing their sensory awareness and motor skills. They learn how to sense the world and take action to meet their needs.

- Pre-Operational: two to seven years

This is when the child will learn how to use symbols to represent real-world events and objects. Symbols are used to represent something and you can have lots of symbols that represent one thing. The child will start to develop a sense of the past and future. This will mark their progression into their next development stage.

An important abstract map that a child will learn is language. Language is a symbolic representation of their world. Once a child has learned to use the symbol, they will be able to communicate their needs to those around them. Children will learn several different symbols so that they can communicate and parents will have differing success levels of being about to interpret their symbols.

- Concrete Operations: seven to eleven years

Operations here refer to logical rules or calculations that can be used to solve problems. The child will be able to understand symbols and change those symbols to figure out problems. At first, this is still going to have to be within the context of real-world situations. When children are taught math at this phase, they will likely do better using objects than purely abstract ideas. About age six is when most children will learn the quantity of something and will remain constant even if the size and shape of a container are different.

- Formal Operations: 12 plus years

The child has started to develop adult thinking abilities, especially the ability to use abstract operations and logic and they will form theories about the way things work.

Once you have a full appreciation of the way the mind develops, you will start to see how learning is a process that is able to be copied and studied. No matter how old we are, what job we have, or our social status, we all have our life to share experiences.

Before we dive headfirst into NLP modeling practices, we need to make sure that you understand a thing or two about learning. Learning is a natural process that modeling tries to unpick and replicate. When you understand the learning process, you will notice that it is easier to use the models.

While most people will spend their entire life learning more and more about their craft, it shouldn't take them a lifetime to master one specific skill in their craft. Most of the learning time will be redundant; working on motor actions instead of actually learning decision criteria or doing things that have an effect on that skill that you want to model.

While there may be several theories out there about learning, representing all of the different ways that you are able to analyze the subject, the one we are going to look at is Kolb's theory because it shows you a cyclical learning process instead of a static one. David Kolb published his learning model in 1984. This was called Kolb's experiential learning theory. He divided the learning cycle into four stages:

1. Concrete Experience

This stage is the visceral, first hand, direct, physical, and real sensory experience. One experience could be made up of any combo of smells, tastes, feelings, sounds, and sights. You might even know that every experience and memories are made up of every element, even though some are likely to be less prominent than others. These concrete experiences are external and will happen in the present.

2. Reflective Observation

After a person has had a concrete experience, they will reflect upon it. The mind is cast back, both unconsciously and consciously, and then relives the experience so that they are able to create generalizations and create conclusions. Research has found that the brain structure called the hippocampus will make an "action replay" of events that were emotionally charged. This will etch them into our long-term memory. Reflective observation is internal and is always in the past. The observation may not always be visual, it uses the sensory information that was there when you had the first experience.

3. Abstract Concept

Once you have relived the experience, you will take the conclusions you have drawn and use them to make an abstract concept. This is a set of principles or rules that govern that experience any other ones like it. When this process involves mental rehearsal, it will be internal and happen in the future, but it is actually a replay of the past that you aren't able to internally represent in the future, so it doesn't exist yet.

4. Active Experiment

Lastly, the abstract concept will be tested by applying it to a new situation. A child will do this by testing out objects they find out the house to see if they float as their balloon did. A man gives the plants in the house a close trim so that he can try out his hedge trimmer that he got as a present. This active experimentation will bring you full circle to a new concrete experience. This will either contradict or affirm the abstract concept. Active experimentation is external and always in the present.

There are some NLP practitioners that would let you think that a model is able to be installed in just a few seconds, but this tends to be unrealistic. Studies on brain plasticity and learning have found that a realistic time to program in a new behavior will take around six months when you practice it daily, reflect, and integrate. It's interesting to see that the most advanced and current work in neuroscience adds more weight to what teachers have been telling us for years now. Students need to have regular practice over a long time period along with proper rest so that they can truly master a skill. Getting a good night's sleep is a part of this learning process.

One common way to approach learning is to have the sequence of activities structured like this:

1. Come up with a theory.
2. Locate practical examples of it.
3. Use this theory to create a personal concept.
4. Apply your personal concept.
5. Reflect on your experience to create a new theory.
6. Repeat the entire process with new, and maybe contradictory, theory.

A student who is studying may learn about Jung's theory of archetypes. They could look at the descriptions and locate real-life examples of people they know that fit into those descriptions. They could use a psychometric instrument or indicator tool to bring their experiences into the process of learning. They would then figure out how they could use this theory in their work and practically use it.

After some time working on the theory, they may reflect on the things they have learned, how it can be practically used, and about their own experiences and preconceptions. They would abstract those experiences and make a new model.

Perspective

There is a famous adage you will likely hear when using NLP: "The map is not the territory." All this means is that you can't understand reality. The only thing that you are able to truly understand is your perception of reality which is based upon your perspective.

Perspective is the thing that gives you an understanding of the world. One person could see the world from one point of view and come up with one perspective. Looking at it from a different point of view, another person will likely come up with a different perspective. This is the same thing that happened to the six blind men and the elephant. This story comes from Wil Dieck's book, *Ordinary People, Extraordinary Lives: The Convergence of Mind, Body, and Spirit*.

These six men lived in a hut in India. A little boy came into the village one day and ran into their hut and told them, "There's an elephant in the village!" The blind men were interested in learning what an elephant looked like since they had never seen one. They all held hands and the boy led them to the elephant that was calmly standing in the middle of the village. The elephant was eating some veggies that the villagers had brought him.

The blind circled him. The one in the front felt the elephant's trunk. He thought the elephant looked like a tree branch. The next man felt its ears and said the elephant was like a fan. The third man felt the elephant's leg. He thought the elephant was like a pillar of the temple. The next man felt the tail and said the elephant was only a tiny tree branch. The fifth felt its side and said the elephant was like the temple's walls. And the last was rubbing the tusks and said that the elephant was a sharp spear.

These men argued loudly. Soon, they started to disturb the villagers. Finally, one of the old men in the village told them to stop. He told the men to move around the elephant and feel all of the elephant.

They respected the man, so they did as he said. Every time they moved, they each experienced a new part of the elephant. This gave them all a different perspective. They were each able to experience things from each other's perspective.

Much like the blind men, you are going to experience the world through your own senses. The information that you receive will be turned into usable data through neurological functions. This data will allow you to make your own reality map. The problem with your map is that you will only see your own reality.

Using NLP, you will be able to examine your map so that you can figure out if your view is accurate, or at the very least, suitable for you to use. If you find that it's not, you will be able to use NLP to change your map. These types of adjustments will give you control over the way you experience the world. It will also provide you with the chance to help others view things from your point of view.

Throughout your life, your mind has created shortcuts that help you to understand the world around you. All of these shortcuts control your focus. The focus is what controls your purpose. These shortcuts are sometimes good, like when you stop a red light or when you look both ways before you walk across the street. Sometimes the shortcuts aren't good. You may hear a song that reminds you of a sad moment. You get the smell of sugar cookies and then you feel like you have to eat one. Of course, you won't be able to only eat one.

NLP will help you to figure out what your shortcuts are so that you can redefine them. This is going to give you better control.

You will also be able to identify another person's shortcuts. You can use this understanding to help them redefine theirs as well.

A perceptual position is a way that a person will see a conversation or interaction. When the perceptional position is varied, you are able to change how you see things. It will also help you to get a better view of another person's perspective.

Negotiations are one of the best uses of perceptional positions. Having a good negotiation is only possible if you understand all viewpoints. With any conflict, the solution will need to take a different perspective. This will give you the chance to see the problem from the other person's perspective. After you understand their perspective, you will be able to notice what they want and why they are going after it. This perspective is what will allow you to provide an acceptable alternative.

There are four different perceptual positions to look at. These four will range from seeing something through your own eyes to seeing an interaction as an outsider.

1. The first perceptual position is being fully associated. This means that you and your body are experiencing things as it happens. You are able to feel, hear, and see through your point of view.

2. The second position is that you feel experiences that somebody else has. This is done by figuratively placing yourself in their shoes. From here, you will be able to think about how that person feels and how they think. This will help you to understand a problem from another person's perspective.

3. The third position is where you observe the interaction or dialogue between the second and first position. From this position, you are able to use what you are

witnessing and hearing to create some assumptions about the other positions. This will give you another way to look at their dynamics and relationship.

4. The fourth position is as a mediator. From here, you are able to address the third position. Here you are trying to figure out if there is another concept that will be helpful. From this point, you will also be able to look at the second position so that you can find other understandings of their behaviors and thoughts. This is going to help you to figure out how you could benefit from them.

These positions are extremely important for NLP. They are used to get clear ideas of the several different perspectives that could be used in any situation at any point. As you move along with these positions, you will start to see your beliefs and values change. These different perceptions will let you learn things you wouldn't have otherwise. You will be able to use these understandings to figure out the best solution.

Take Charge of Your Mind

The Rule of Expectations will use expectations to impact reality and get results. People will make decisions on the way they think others want them to perform. Because of this, people will fulfill these expectations whether they are negative or positive. Expectations have impacts on people we respect and trust, but a bigger impact on strangers. If we realize that somebody is expecting something from us, we try to satisfy them to gain likability and respect.

We've all heard the saying: "What gets measured, gets done." This is also true when talking about expectations. What is expected is what will happen. People will do whatever possible to meet your expectations. This force is powerful and could lead to either the destruction or improvement of this person. You might be expressing expectations of skepticism, lack of confidence, or doubt and you will get results. If you think highly of a person, show them confidence, and want them to succeed, and you will see results from them. To quote John H. Spalding: "Those who believe in our ability do more than stimulate us. They create for us an atmosphere in which it becomes easier to succeed." Once you have created expectations, you will change a person's behavior. When we label certain characters or behaviors, this action is expected. If these expectations aren't met, you might see dissatisfaction, surprise, disgust, or anger.

We can communicate expectations in many different ways. It could be through body language, voice inflections, or language. Think about a time when you were introduced to a new person. If they give you their first name, you give them yours. If they give their full name, you do the same. You might not even realize it, you are accepting cues from them regarding their expectations and you are acting according to their wishes. We all unknowingly send out expectations and cues. Their power is by using the Rule of Expectations consciously.

Many studies have shown how expectations can influence other's performance in drastic ways. In one study, they told a classroom of kids that no one was going to do well on the test and everyone did poorly on the test. In another study, assembly workers were told their job was hard and didn't perform as well on the same task as the workers who were told it was an easy job. Another study showed adults that were given mazes solved them faster when they were told they were grade school level mazes.

If you can add the Rule of Expectations to your repertoire, you could change the audience's expectations of you and their expectation to purchase your idea, service, or product. When you can do this, you will be a lot more persuasive.

Everyone has heard about the Pavlov's dog experiments. Pavlov used the Rule of Expectations to train his dogs to begin salivating when they heard a buzzer. The Rule of Expectations has been used in advertising to make us humans salivate when we see commercials or think about a specific food.

Expect with Confidence

Sometimes we base our expectations on what we assume about groups of people or an individual person. This is the same with us. You may have noticed how expectations have become a reality in your life. Expectations are a self-fulfilled prophecy. We accomplish this by subconsciously and consciously. If there was a child in school with you who were constantly disruptive and rowdy, people have already assumed them to act in a specific way and that is how they will act. They may not even mean to act this way. This child knew everyone thought he was disruptive and so he became disruptive. His teachers expected bad behavior and their expectations were fulfilled.

Think about the impact this might have in your life. Do the expectations and assumptions you have about yourself victimize or liberate you? There are numerous examples of the Rule of Expectations working each day. Have you noticed a person who thought they were getting fired? Their enthusiasm and quality of work dropped. What happens next? They got fired. Their belief caused them to act in a specific way. Those expectations then work to do the very thing they were worried about.

A study was done with second graders who listened to their teachers before they took a math test. They heard three types of statements — reinforcement, persuasion, or expectation. The reinforcement statements went something like this: "You've done excellent work." "I'm happy about your progress." The persuasion statements said: "You need to get better grades in math." "You should be good at math." The expectation statements said: "You work hard at math." "You know math very well." What do you think the results looked like? The expectation statements had the highest scores. Why were these most effective? They gave each student personal assumptions. These assumptions conditioned the results.

Expectation Affect Behavior

When we create expectations for others, they usually become reality. This has interesting effects when we apply them to the real world. Let's go over some examples of how expectations can change lives and persuade behaviors of people.

- School Teachers

When talking about expectations, teachers could be the worst negative influence or the best asset for a child. If a teacher labels a student as being a troublemaker, it will create specific expectations on the student's actions. Labels such as "ADD", "stupid", "slow learner" can become projections on a child's future success. I remember a story about a substitute teacher who received a note from the normal teacher telling her about that there was one student who always caused trouble and another who was very helpful. As the substitute started class, she looked for these students. Once she found them, she treated them as their labels stated. Once the teacher came back, it amazed her that the substitute found the troublemaker was very helpful and the helper was a troublemaker. The substitute mixed them up. The children behaved based on the substitute's expectation. This is also referred to as social labeling. People will live up to either the negative or positive label that gets put on them.

Everyone has had teachers who expected great things from us and brought us to another level. Can you even imagine how powerful this can be? Think about the first day of class while the teacher is looking around the room. Let's say she has a student who is the offspring of a well-known Asian professor, another one is the sister of a former class clown, and one who has many piercings and is wearing nothing but black. You can probably imagine what her expectations and assumptions were. Her expectations will be fulfilled without even talking to any of the students.

One experiment shows how the teacher's expectations can influence students. An elementary school chose two Head Start teachers who were equals in practice and potential. Then, the classes were formed by students who had been tested to make sure they were very similar in learning potential and background. The principal talked to the teachers alone. He gave the first teacher a pep talk and told her she was very fortunate to have a class of very potential students for the year. "Don't get in their way, let them run." The other teacher was told her students weren't very bright but to do the best she could with them. At the conclusion of the school year, the classes were tested and it wasn't surprising to find the first class scored higher than the second. The only factor that was different was the teacher's expectations.

- Grubby Day

Most schools will have days where students were allowed to dress up for Halloween, Fifties Day, Pajama Day, or Spirit Day. One high school had a day labeled as Grubby Day. As you might have guessed, during this day, student's behaviors were not very outstanding. The administrators received more complaints on the student's behaviors during this day than any other. This dress code set up specific assumptions that set up specific expectations. These expectations became fulfilled by bad behavior.

- Littering

Most children will always drop their trash on the floor. One elementary teacher gave her students individually wrapped pieces of candy. The majority of the wrappers wound up on the floor instead of the garbage can. During the next few weeks, the teacher made a point of telling her students how tidy and neat the students had been. The principal came to visit this class and commented on the fact that this class was the cleanest and neatest in the entire school. The janitor even wrote a note on the chalkboard and told the students how clean their room was. When the two weeks were up, the children were given candy again. This time, the wrappers were put into the trash.

- Parental Expectation

The main thing to notice about small children and toddlers is they will behave according to what their parents expect of them. While interning in college and visiting various playgrounds learning about children's behaviors, I noticed that if a child fell down or bumped into another child, they automatically looked to their parent to see how they were going to react. If the parent showed pain or concern on their face, their child would begin to cry to get attention. This happened whether or not the child was really hurt. Any time my daughter would fall around my mother, my mother would automatically fall apart and my daughter would begin to cry uncontrollably. It didn't matter if she was hurt bad or not. The crying began and it would take a long time to get her calmed back down.

A technique I tried was opposite of this approach. I changed expectations and it worked wonderfully. If my child hit her head or scraped her knee, she looked at me and I would ask her if she was bleeding. When she looked at her injury and didn't see blood, she would smile and continue playing. If she saw blood, she would become concerned but we would wash it off, bandage it up and she would be playing again in a matter of minutes.

Children will always live up to their parent's expectations whether these are negative or positive. Most of the inmates in prison were told by their parents while growing up, "You are going to go to jail." Guess what, they did.

- Blood Drive

Blood drive organizers will make calls to remind donors to come in. They usually end their conversations by stating something like, "We will see you in the morning at ten am, okay?" They will wait for the person's commitment before they hang up. Why do they do it this way? Studies show when you make an expectation toward someone, the attendance rate will go up tremendously.

- Sales Applications

Power of suggestions is a very effective way to engage emotions into your tactics. When a car salesperson states: "You are really going to fall in love with this car because it can handle these mountain roads very well." He is taking the focus off the sale and creating an image in the buyer's head. He is speaking as they have already agreed on the same since you won't be driving the roads if you haven't bought the car. He is acting as if it is a done deal. The truth of the matter is the more he talks like this, the more it will probably happen.

Salespeople who go door to door have to use this law. They walk up to a door, ring the bell, and plaster a huge smile on their face while telling this potential buyer they have a presentation that they absolutely have to see. They are employing this strategy while wiping their dirty feel on the doormat hoping to be asked into the house. It is surprising that this technique still continues to work. You can see the salesperson giving the purchaser a pen hoping they are going to sign a contract. Have you felt bad when you leave a store and didn't buy anything? The store created an expectation that you will buy something.

Your Inner Voice

It doesn't matter what we call it. Some call it wisdom, soul, insight, knowledge, or gut feeling. This is what we all look for.

A simple definition of intuition is "The ability to understand something immediately, without the need for conscious reasoning."

It might be a sixth sense, inkling, feeling, or hunch. It is the way we make judgments and snap decisions. We've all had an intuition, feeling, or hunch and even though there wasn't any evidence to back up these feelings, data and science did back up what they already knew to be true.

Most of our brain activity will happen on unconscious levels. Studies show that five percent of our cognitive activity like behavior, actions, emotions, and decisions will come from the conscious mind.

We take in information through our senses every second of every day and we process it all at very fast speeds. That voice, sense, inkling, hunch, intuition is coming from loads of information that we can't consciously or cognitively process.

A simple definition of cognition is "The mental action or process of acquiring knowledge and understanding through our senses, experiences, and thoughts."

This is talking about organizing, discernment, problem-solving, and understanding. This is the thinking and logical part of our brains. We constantly weigh cons and pros, coming to rational conclusions that are based on factors or data. These are the voices that try to override our instincts.

What if I Don't Hear Voices?

Your inner wisdom isn't always a voice you hear. Sometimes it might be an emotion, energy, image, sensation, or feeling. You might feel it in your body. There is no right or wrong way to experience this inner voice. The main thing is to figure out where and when you feel it.

- Gut Feeling

Do you feel it in your gut? You might have heard our guts are our second brain. This is due to the enteric nervous system. It operates separately from the spinal cord, brain, and central nervous system. Yes, you can think with your gut.

Marisa Peer has stated: "The stomach is the seat of all emotions and your feeling are the most real thing you have; so the trick is to listen to your feelings. If something feels wrong, your inner voice is saying it is not right for you. If you get the horrible lurch in your stomach, your inner voice is telling you it is wrong."

- Heart

I asked a good colleague and friend who has always had a good sense of self-awareness where her inner voice is, she replied: "My heart. It is always my heart." This isn't surprising since our hearts are intelligent organs.

Many people don't realize that our hearts can decide, think, and feel for itself. It has about 40,000 neurons and a complete network of neurotransmitters that have very specific functions. This makes it the perfect extension of your brain. It is automatic like a primal, mysterious voice is telling us that the center of our conscience and true being is located there.

- Head

When talking to a male friend about their inner voice, they balked at the idea of the feeling being in his heart or gut. He told me that his inner voice was always in the back of his head that will talk to him and not with him.

Dropping Anchors

Everybody has been faced with a mound of work to accomplish and you end up feeling lazy and overwhelmed. You find it hard to kick-start your mind. The problem is that we view our workload in a boring light. Because we associate it like this, our body will respond by slowing down out actions and creating a sleep-like state. This will cause you to get lost in doing something else and your work will continue to pile up.

We have the power to change our body's response to a thing by changing our emotions associated with that task. This will make us more productive. This technique is referred to as anchoring. This method will recall previous positive experiences and associate it with what is currently happening.

Anchoring can be used in several situations — at work, during a presentation, moments before an interview, during a performance, meeting a person, going on a date, and so on. You can view it as copying and pasting a positive emotion that you need. This can be done first thing in the morning to prepare you for your day.

1. Mental prep

Find a quiet place. Peace is important, so distractions should be eliminated to reap the most benefits. Relax and allow your heartbeat to slow. Cancel out the out world and close your eyes.

2. Recall a previous positive experience

This can be anything as long as that moment makes you feel good when you think about it. Take ten seconds to remember all of the details. This will normally work better when you can use all five of your senses. Think about what you heard, felt, smelled, the other people around, and what you looked at.

3. Associate with an action

Keep this memory in your mind. As you do this, perform an action. The easiest action is to squeeze the thumb and index fingers of your right hand. While you do this, increase the feelings that are flowing through you. Make sure that you make the picture vivid and alive.

This is what is known as laying the anchor. When you recalled your event, you use neurological components that created emotions to come up. By squeezing your fingers, you created a bookmark in your mind. Now you will associate that finger squeeze with a happy memory.

4. Repeat

Take a few minutes and perform your action at least five times more. You want to make sure that your mind quickly connects the action with your happy memory. With practice, that squeeze will flash an image of happiness into your mind.

5. Use your anchor

Before you do something that you are dreading, you can use your anchor to provide you with confidence to do well. When you do use your anchor, increase those feelings and then quickly break your state once the memories are at their peak. By cutting off your anchor right before it peaks, the energy will hang around. Open your eyes and you will notice a surge of positivity.

Breaking state can be done by doing a random act like looking at something around you or reading a text.

Another way to use anchors is to replace a negative emotion with a positive emotion. Remember, you need to practice this method and the one before to get the best results.

1. Anchor your negative memory

Like before, relax, close your eyes, and recall a negative experience. You want to make it real, but not overpowering. Too much power could make things worse. Use a gesture on your left hand to create the anchor. Recall this anchor a couple of times to make sure that you can feel this negative moment. Break your state for 30 seconds.

2. Use your positive anchor

Try to think of a moment that had you feeling the opposite of your negative anchor. This is where you need to focus. Increase this memory. Let this moment meditate in your mind for 30 seconds. Try to remember every little detail. Create an action on your right hand for this anchor.

3. Test your positive anchor

When you perform the gesture for the positive anchor, you want that mental image to become huge. You want your emotions to intensify. Let everything else go and let those feelings consume you. Do the step two to three times then break state.

4. Collapse the anchors

This is tricky and will need some practice. Your positive anchor needs to have a more intense effect than the negative one. Take a deep breath and relax. When you're ready, activate both of your anchors at the exact same time. It's going to feel weird because your brain won't like feeling these contrasting emotions together. Since your positive anchor is more intense, it is going to overpower your negative one and cause it to collapse. After the positive state has taken over, hold onto it for ten seconds. Open your eyes and you will notice a surge of positivity.

Dissociation

A powerful controller is an association-dissociation pattern. You want to take a vacation but you need to save up some money first. What will make you save money?

- Association

You think about your destination as a movie. You see it in 3D and it feels like you can reach out and touch it. You hear sounds and music. You hear a rhythm. It feels like you are really there, seeing it with your own eyes. Deep down there is a fear. When we get overwhelmed with emotions, dissociating is a great relief.

- Dissociation

You are thinking about your destination but only see a small black and white photo. You may see yourself there instead of seeing it with your eyes. This inner voice tells you "I guess it might be nice."

- Using Association Dissociation

This pattern is an important submodality distinction. When we are associated, we relive an experience and feel all the feeling. When we are dissociated, we see ourselves. The feelings we have are about the experience. This is not the same thing as the mental health "Dissociative Disorders".

- When to be associated

If you are remembering or experiencing something pleasant, it would be great to be associated. It is a necessary part of learning a new skill such as a physical activity like sports. It's a great way to get motivated and to enjoy activities.

- When to be dissociated

It is more useful to dissociate yourself from unpleasant experiences and memories. How can you get motivated to do a time consuming or unpleasant task? You have to view yourself doing everything associated with the task and follow it through to an end result. Focus on feelings of a task well done.

- Making life miserable

Most people will do the opposite. They will continuously experience unpleasant events or memories in a way that you experience all the bad feelings. They will remember good events in a totally disconnected way. It is horrible to do something fun but you aren't experiencing all the joys of it. You are thinking about your taxes.

Content Reframing

Content reframing refers to a consciously directed form of a positive attitude that will enable you to get the best outcome from the worst situations. It gives you the chance to reframe the content of a negative moment into something more positive.

To help you learn how to reframe, we're going to look at a common occurrence, the unexpected loss of a job. When you lose a job, everything will look bleak. It may not be all that easy to find another position. While all of this happens, you still have to face the realities of life.

But you can look at this in a different way. Since you are out of work, you know of new opportunities to find a better job. You can explore different skills and opportunities that you may not have thought of before. It will also build character. You will become more courageous, daring, and self-reliant.

With this, you have attempted to reframe your negative event into a positive outcome. It will be surprising to notice all of your blind spots that negative emotions can cause. Content reframing gives you a chance to step back, take a breath, and view your situation from a more objective place.

Content reframing doesn't deny the fact that your situation will be difficult, but you will be more likely to face the situation more successfully if you view it as a moment of growth.

The Art of Persuasion and Manipulation

Meta-programs are the way you internally represent your experiences. They are mental shortcuts or recognition patterns. They work to sort out and prioritize what your body senses. This can help you make sense of the information you have received.

The term meta came from computer science. It is derived from the way a program can control the functions of another program.

Another way to think about meta-programs is in biological terms. Here's an example: Hormones that are produced in the pituitary gland can control the hormones that are produced in various glands in the endocrine system.

Meta-program is a way of thinking that changes how you look at reality. These can control your focus, actions, behaviors, and decisions.

These are processes that are subconsciously in your mind. They manage and direct other processes that happen at either meta or elevated levels.

Our brains can use strategies for decision making and being convinced of things. These are internal processes and mental representation that get made up from input from the five senses.

When making decisions, a person might go through several unconscious thoughts such as first you might see images of different options. Second, after you have had time to examine them, you may see that some have possibilities. Then you can choose one that feels best to you.

This is called "kinesthetic, auditory-internal, visual-constructed" in NLP talk. This happened because you saw the image visually and then figured out how you felt about it.

Somebody else could have feelings for each choice first and then see how each one might be implemented and figure out which one they want. Practitioners of NLP call this sequence: kinesthetic is when you feel the choices; visual-constructed is where you see the choices working and then auditory-internal is where you tell yourself the choice.

If two people use the exact strategy, they might come up with totally different results. One person could come to a decision. The other person could feel overwhelmed and confused and not make a decision.

Meta-programs were created from trying to discover what created different responses. Because the internal process is the same, the differences were thought to come from outside sources. These sources were "meta to" the internal process.

What causes this to happen? Our brains are constantly taking in infinite numbers of sensations. Our conscious mind is just capable of being aware of around seven items at any one time. Our brains would be completely overwhelmed if we were completely aware of every single thing at one time.

But all this can lead to other problems. What parts of specific data needs to be selected? What should we pay attention to right now?

In order to work effectively, our minds need to sort out and select just one thing from all the things we are receiving. This is called sorting.

This brings us to another question. How do our subconscious minds make the choices that will give us the best option at that moment?

Habitual Thinking

There are two facts when talking about thinking. One, most of our thinking is habitual. Two, we filter out most of what we receive. To be truthful, most of the input will get no attention at all.

Do you need proof? At this moment, what does the blood that is flowing in your right arm feel like? You hadn't paid any attention to it until this very moment.

Most of the time, just like your arm, filtering is good. What do you do if your subconscious is choosing the wrong information? Information that isn't beneficial at this very moment in time?

What if the meta-program is filtering something that might be helpful, things that you could really use?

If you can gain access to your meta-programs, what would it feel like? Would you be able to make more informed and better decisions and choices?

Scientists first assumed that these programs were already hard-wired into our brains. Others wanted to see if NLP could be used to change them.

Research has shown that meta-programs can be changed by mapping experiences together. They figured out a process that let people "try out" this new program before making it a new habit. By doing this, we only adopt changes that were compatible with other aspects of the personality.

Meta-Programs of NLP

It depends on which expert you ask as to how many meta-programs NLP has. One scientist identified 60, another 51. Don't worry, we are only going to cover four.

- To or Away

This program answers the question of what motivates a person. Is it pleasure or pain? Do you move to feelings of pleasure or away from pain? You could also think about this as where our attention is directed. Is it to what you want or away from what you don't want?

Use this to look at yourself. Do you move toward pleasure or away from pain? If you are a person who moves away from, you think about things in the perspective as to what needs to be avoided. Threats energize you. After you have read an article on diabetes, you might think, "If I don't lose weight and cut back on sugar, I'll become diabetic." This focus causes you to take action by moving away from the pain of getting diabetes.

You get motivated through ways to reach your goals. Think back to the article on diabetes. You will now tell yourself, "If I can improve my weight by exercise and diet, I will be healthier." You aren't moving away from diabetes but you are pushing yourself to good health.

A good way to understand a preference is the way you approach a problem. If you are an away person, you will express and think in terms of what you don't want. If they are asked what you want, you will probably answer like this: "Well, I don't want that to happen and I don't want this. I know this isn't going to help me either."

You are moving away from the pain you are feeling and

experiencing. If you are a to person, when someone asks what you want, you might answer: "I would like to feel better, more focused, stronger, etc."

- Frame of Reference

This gives you that answers as to where your motivation comes from. Is it externally or internally? This is called your locus of control.

Your frame of reference will answer this question: "Do you rate your performance from internal standards or do you find feedback from other people?"

If your frame of reference is internal, you get motivation from inside your body. These standards are what you use to judge performance. You usually feel that your outcome is a result of your actions. This is also called an internal locus of control.

If your frame of reference is external, you get motivated by receiving feedback from the world. You use other people's feedback to judge how well you did something. This is called an external locus of control.

If your frame of reference is external, you experience life as it happens to you. You think other people's actions have control over what you accomplish. You find the advice of experts and are influenced by thoughts of others.

- Match Vs. Mismatch

In this program, your attention gets focused on what is different or the same. Do you see things that are similar, alike, or have things in common, or contrast, dislikes, or differences?

One aspect of thinking is our brains are designed to find differences. When we don't notice the same thing happening over and over is called having a habit. This process lets us determine if something hasn't changed enough to grab our attention. By doing this we get to leave it out of our consciousness and focus attention elsewhere.

Being "different" definitely gets our attention. This is because, after thousands and thousands of generations, we figured out that something different could actually mean danger. Being able to see "different" is needed to survive.

We can also see this concept in language. If we would like to express our affection for others, we tell them we "like" them. If we have negative feelings toward somebody, we will say we "dislike" them.

- Possibility or Necessity?

Our behaviors are based on necessity. Others behave based on what could be possible, what might work in their lives.

If possibilities motivate you, you look for the good in the situation. You can see the opportunities. You think you have control and choice about the direction of your life.

If necessity motivates you, you will focus on things you need to do. This may include staying late after everyone has gone home because you feel like you "have to" get all the work done before you can leave. You focus only on the consequences of what will happen if you don't finish.

When motivated by necessity, a person will just do what they need to. They feel as if they don't have any choices. Their world is made up of constraints and rules.

Think about this, why do certain people apply for specific jobs?

Some will apply due to necessity. They feel as if there aren't any other options for them. This means they have to act in a specific way.

Others will apply just because it makes them feel in control of their lives. This person may be motivated by what they want to achieve. These people don't focus on what they "feel" they need to do.

- Sorting

While using meta-programs, you will be working on sorting things out. Sorting will help you choose things from a large group. When you are working for others or yourself, you will be able to target certain attitudes. These can be found while talking to people.

When using meta-programs, you will get in tune with yourself. You could also use them to understand what makes others tick. This will improve how well you interact with people you meet every day.

Internal Representation

We are aware of what happens around us by using our five senses. When we memorize, remember, dream, or think, we are using these senses. We use these to reproduce information we get from sources. These senses are a medium for input.

This includes our smells, tastes, feelings, dialogue, sounds, and internal pictures. Something comes through our input channels that are:

- Gustatory: This is our taste or the ability to know the difference between salty, bitter, sour, and sweet in our mouths.

- Olfactory: This is smell or the ability to distinguish scents.

- Kinesthetic: This is the external or internal feeling that includes touching something or someone, our emotions, textures, and pressures.

- Auditory: This includes sounds, what we heard, and the way people talk.

- Visual: This includes what we see or how somebody looks at us.

We use these systems or mainly the three most used one of feeling, hearing, and seeing all the time and in everything we do. Some of these we aren't even aware of when we do them. Our minds experience things either unconsciously or consciously by tastes, smells, feelings, sounds, and pictures as our senses see the objective world.

Our internal feelings, sounds, and pictures that all of us experience are very likely to be different because of our individual interpretations. These differences cause us to think differently and have various states of mind. We don't know what others think about us but we always think we know. We might watch the same film and conclude that everyone else will agree that it is boring. This isn't always the case. The main reason is the difference in our thinking preference. They are the different senses we use inwardly.

Everyone has a preference to which sense they use in the outer world, the way to communicate, or the way they think. Some people like pictures and images. They remember faces better than sounds. These people have a visual preference. The other will have an auditory preference as they find it easier to remember names through introductions.

People will unintentionally reveal their preference by using certain words like: "I **see** what you mean" suggests this person has a visual preference. "Your idea **sounds** wonderful" suggests this person has an auditory preference. "These shoes **feel** great on my feet" suggests a kinesthetic preference. A person wanting to purchase a new car will be willing to listen to salespeople, some might want to look through the car, and some feel better if they can feel the car. Everyone unconsciously uses their senses each day. It is normal to have a dominant preference.

Since we use all our senses all the time, external experiences will come to mind through all our systems. Because of a preference or what we like to do, we have senses that are more advanced than others when responding to the world. A football fan that regularly goes to games uses mostly their eyes. They will have a very developed visual system. A person who goes to the movies a lot will use their auditory and visual senses. Thinking normally involves the three primary representational systems, kinesthetic, auditory, and visual, many people will favor one or two no matter what they are thinking about.

We can get many benefits from knowing our representational systems. Basic understanding could enable us to be the master of our own mind. We can gain control over the way we view inputs from the world. This will influence our behavior and feelings in the way we choose instead of being subjected to external influences. If we try to identify and use someone else's primary system, we will actually communicate with them better. When we use a common system, it will enhance and facilitate mutual understanding.

After we have figured out our primary system, we can identify our potential. People that display skills in a certain field will have a well-developed representational system. A person who has a visual preference might take up interior design or painting. A person who has an auditory preference might have a career in public speaking or teaching. A person with a kinesthetic preference might have a choice in being either a chef or hair stylist. A person who has an underdeveloped auditory system may have problems playing musical instruments. Some people are quick to conclude they have no talent for a certain activity when their primary sense just hasn't been developed yet.

An external event comes in by a sensory input channel and gets filtered and managed by our nervous system. As we manage the way we perceive these, we generalize, distort, and delete information according to the processes that help to filter our perception.

Everyone has the same five systems but we all differ in the way we see the world internally. With time, we figure out our unique way of using our mental maps. It is a good way to talk to a crowd using combinations of these systems.

Communication Model

- Deletion

This happens when we pay attention to specific parts of an experience and not others. We sometimes omit or overlook others. If our brains didn't delete some information, we would be facing too much information. You might feel as if you have been overloaded with information.

- Distortion

This happens when we change reality by making changes to our experience in sensory data. An old Indian fable about snake analogy versus the distortion of a rope goes like this: A man walking saw what he thought to be a snake and he yells "SNAKE". When he arrived at the place in the road, he discovered that what he thought was a snake was just a piece of rope.

This is an important component of the Communication Model and is used to motivate ourselves. Motivation could happen when we corrupt, change or misrepresent what comes into our nervous system. This information gets changes through a filtering system.

- Generalization

This is where we draw conclusions about several experiences. You might even know somebody who has experienced something one time and form an opinion based on that one time such as "I hate all Country music because I listened to Taylor Swift and I didn't like the way she sang."

Normally, our conscious mind can handle about seven pieces of information at one time. If it gets overloaded, so we try to oversimplify our attitudes and decisions based on information that didn't give enough evidence. Generalization is common today. Everyone does it. It is the result of digital information that causes overload and takes over our sensibility.

We know several people who can't handle seven. If you want to try someone out ask them to name more than seven products in specific categories. Most people might be able to name two or three products in a low-interest category and around nine in a high-interest category. There is the reasoning behind this.

If we don't delete information, we will have too much information coming in. In fact, you might have heard psychologists say that if we were aware of all the information that came in, we might go crazy. This is why we filter all information.

Generalization is the best way we can learn. We take the information we have and then draw conclusions about these conclusions. The main question is when two people receive the same stimulus, don't they have the same response? The answer is basically we generalize and delete information that comes into one of our five filters. These filters are as follows:

- *Programs*

The first of these filters is Programs. When you know a person's program, you can predict a person's state, behaviors, and actions. Programs aren't bad or good, that is just the way somebody handles information.

- *Values*

Values are basically an evaluation filter. This is how we decide if our actions are bad or good, wrong or right and the way we feel about these actions. Values are arranged in a hierarchy with the one that is most important being on the top and the ones that don't matter is lower than that. Everyone has different models of the world. Our values are the result of the way we look at the world. If we communicate with somebody else or ourselves, or if our model of the world conflicts with values whether they are ours or someone else's, there will be conflict.

Values are what we normally move away from or to. This is what repulses or attracts us to something. They are an unconscious, deep belief system about what is important. Values can also change with context. You may have specific values about what you want out of a relationship and what you want in your business. Your values about one will be different than the other. Actually, if they aren't, you might have trouble with both. Because values are related to context, they might be related to the state.

- *Beliefs*

Beliefs are how we generalize about the world. Beliefs are the way we assume the world to be. Whether it denies or creates personal power. Beliefs are basically our on and off switches. When we are working with somebody else's beliefs, we have to discover what they believe that causes them to do the things they do. We also need to know any disabling beliefs that don't let them do what they want to do.

- *Memories*

Many psychologists say the present only plays a small part in our behavior. They think that as we age, our reactions now are just reactions to collections of memories that we have organized of past memories. We can make changes to our memories to get more positive results.

- *Decisions*

Decisions that we made in our past could create new beliefs or might affect our perception with time. The problem with decisions is that they can be made either at an early age or unconsciously are forgotten. The effect still remains. We can make changes to our decisions.

These filters will determine how we view an event that is happening now. It is the way we represent what puts us into a certain state and physiology. Whatever state we might be in determines our behavior and the communication model determines the way we process information from the world outside.

Three Components of NLP

You can learn more about NLP by focusing on three central components. These are as follows:

1. Subjectivity

Every person will experience the world subjectively. This means that our world experiences make us form subjective models of the way things are. These experiences are comprised of our five senses and our language.

These experiences are formed by our senses of gestation, olfaction, tactician, audition, and vision. By using language, we can think and talk about these experiences. These experiences have patterns that influence the way we view, talk about, and behave in the world.

Our behavior is controlled by these representations. If we can manipulate these subjective experiences, we could possibly change our behavior.

2. Consciousness

Our consciousness branches into two notions —the unconscious and conscious components. Everyone experiences things in our unconscious mind. Our unconscious representation could damage our conscious behavior.

3. Learning

Learning is an imitative behavior and many call this modeling. The theory says that imitative learning could reproduce and code any behavior.

Analyzing Body Language and the Mind

As humans, we are constantly communicating. This could be with hand positions, posture, facial expressions, the tone of voice, words, or if you choose to respond to an email or text message. When you meet a person for the first time, you will probably observe their body movements before they ever speak. At this point, you are sizing up each other. This is so that you can figure out each other's personalities even before you start to talk.

Even though it may be cliché, but actions speak louder than words. Research has found that it takes around four minutes for a person to make their first impression. This means you have a short time period to create a good impression. Surprisingly, you don't have to use your words all that much to create that all too important first impression. Humans will judge each other 55% based solely on body language. The manner of speaking accounts for 38% and the content of their words make up 7%. Even the tone of voice and rhythm is more important than the words that you say.

Before we dive into the different body languages, we are going to quickly look at the way the brain is wired. The brain is made up of two hemispheres. The left hemisphere takes care of the logical data processing. This is what controls the conscious thinking. The right hemisphere is where the emotions are triggered by activity in this area. This hemisphere is also what controls our creativity and intuition.

Since our body is cross-wired, the right hemisphere is what controls the life side of your body, and the left hemisphere controls the right side. This means that any body language shown on a certain side corresponds with the hemisphere of the brain that activates it. Any action that happens on the left side is conscious actions, while actions on the right side are unconscious.

Understanding Body Language

The first stop along the road of body language is facial language. Facial expressions are the first things that a person will notice. A person's mood can be easily noticed depending on how tense or relaxed the facial muscles are. Eyelids even show powerful information.

- Smiling

You can easily notice the feelings using the mouth as a reference point. A smile is typically connected with interest and happiness. A person that smiles too much could be used to hide disinterest. An exaggerated smile shows courtesy or assurance to the speaker to let them know that they are listening even if they aren't. A frown will show dissatisfaction and sadness. Frowning is an unlikely expression when people first meet. This is because we would rather hide our real sentiments instead of being rude. A straight expression or poker face shows neutrality and seriousness. Think about the expression you are interested in giving off the next time that you speak.

- Chin

You can also notice sentiments by checking how they are using their chin. Chin-stroking is a good sign of careful studying. People will often view this as a show of skepticism. Now, if they scratch their chin, it could mean they are confused.

- Jaw and Nostrils

Nostrils are a big indicator of mood or temperament. Heavy breathing with flared nostrils normally means they are angry. It's important that you are aware of these signs. These people should be approached with a soft tone. Don't try to force them to open up when they don't want to. Instead, try giving them some space for a bit before you engage with them again. Another good indicator of their temperament is their jaw muscles. The jaw will normally be in sync with your nostrils. Anger and impatience are typically noticed by the pumping and flexing of the muscles of the jaw.

- Eyes

While eyes are technically a part of facial non-verbal communication, they need to be looked at on their own. Ophthalmic refers to the communication shown by the eyes. This is an effective tool to detect sentiment and mood. People tend to be oblivious to the fact that their eyes share quite a bit of information.

The amount of white you can see under the colored part of the eye, the iris, can reveal how much stress they are feeling at that moment. The white area on the left eye shows the stress the right hemisphere is experiencing. This means that the person could be under stress from the body like lack of food or sleep.

The right eye will show stress from an external source. If the white part of the eye under the iris is revealed after they are exposed to stressful concepts such as overtime and deadlines, the person is likely experiencing discomfort from those things.

Eyelids also show a person's optimism. Watch their bottom lid to see their reaction to your words. If their bottom lid straightens, they are probably skeptical. Once you gain their trust, the bottom lid will round out. This means that they are opening up to you and that you are building rapport.

- Hands and Arms

As we travel down the body, we will start to notice more information about how a person feels. The hands are the main tools for humans, so we will often subconsciously use our hands to express how we feel. These appendages hold more nerves that are connected with our brain than any other body part.

The hands are able to show shyness, anxiety, or restraint if they are being held together. This is due to the energy that is being held between the hands. This is why this is a good way to channel negative energy like nervousness and anger.

If their hands are in the shape of a triangle, the hands are showing deep thinking or confidence. Another variation of this is a rhombus shape where the thumbs are extended out further towards a person. The German Chancellor Angela Merkel is popular for using this gesture. Because of this, the gesture has been given the name the Merkel rhombus that will create a calm yet serious aura.

When you raise your arms with your palms open shows acceptance and honesty. The opposite form shows defiance.

When people give a contemplative look while they use their hands to cover their mouth, they have an idea but they want to keep it to themselves. It helps to encourage these people to share what they are thinking. This could be all they need to make the conversation better.

The manner in which a person crosses their arms will also show their confidence. A partial cross is how a person can unconsciously soothe their own nerves. People who are exhibiting this behavior likely feel anxious. Try easing the mood by making them laugh is some way.

Fully crossed arms will often show that they have an unwillingness to cooperate and work. If they are holding their arms, they are trying to preserve their internal emotions.

- Foot Communication

The feet tend to get ignored when it comes to reading a person's body language. On the contrary, the feet tend to be one of the more candid forms of body language. When people lie, they often hide this by altering their movements. They will focus on their face without realizing their feet are giving them away.

By watching the way that a person sits, you can figure out whether the person is submissive or dominant. Men will normally want to be seen as dominant, this is why they normally take up a lot of space when they sit. They will normally sit with their legs spread apart or in a figure four position. Women tend to be more reserved, so they will cross their legs to take up less space.

Legs will also show a person's sincerity while they are listening. When people want to listen, their legs will point towards the person who is talking with their feet off by a 45-degree angle. However, if their legs are pointing towards the exit, they are not interested in what the person is saying. Make sure you pay attention to the direction of your feet when you are talking.

Reading a person's body language will help you to figure out how to approach them in the friendliest way possible.

Meta Model

How can somebody become better at something? Find a person who is already good at the thing that they want to do and then copy what they do. Modeling is a lot like copying, but copying takes things a bit further. Instead of just copying the observed behavior, it attempts to help a person understand the reasons behind their actions. It's their mental model that will help you to find the same success. Modeling works because it creates a series of templates that are based on things like:

- Physiology
- Body movement
- How people use their language
- All other sensory-related things that a person could notice

This modeling process came about as a result of John Grinder and Richard Bandler's research. The founders of NLP were working to achieve some of the same therapeutic results that Virginia Satir and Fritz Perls were able to achieve. They discovered that they had to do more than just copy their behaviors. They also had to understand their thought processes affected the outcome.

They discovered that those therapists used all of their skills unconsciously. The same is true for pretty much anybody who performs at an extremely high level. This applies to business people all the way to athletes. High performers will not think consciously about what they do. If you ask any of them how they do something, they will likely have a pretty hard time explaining how they did it.

Why is this? Because they've performed these behaviors hundreds of times. They did them so many times that they happen below their conscious thought. They are now automatic. This is why it is almost impossible for the expert to explain their success. This is why modeling is helpful.

Modeling will involve uncovering the things that an expert knows consciously and unconsciously. This is why modeling is so powerful. Models can be used to transfer the successful behaviors, attitudes, and beliefs of one person to yourself. This is what will let you produce the same results.

There are six stages of modeling.

1. Find your model and watch the behavior you are interested in acquiring.

First, you need to find a person who has consistently produced the results you are looking for. For example, you could be interested in modeling a black belt's sparring method. Modeling can be used to duplicate an eloquent public speaker's ability to connect with the audience.

Modeling can also be used for mundane purposes. You could model a person who does a great job at keeping their home clean. You could even model the way that your boss is able to do their "to-do" list. You would also be able to find out why a person stays depressed. The same goes for people who are always frustrated or angry. This knowledge can help you to stay out of this state.

The key is to find a person who is getting a result that you want to produce. They do this in a consistent manner without fail and then you observe the things they do.

2. Unconsciously start to use their behavioral patterns.

In the majority of modeling methods, the modeler will act as an observer. NLP modeling requires that the modeler will step into the successful person's shoes. Through practice and repeated imitation, you will start to unconsciously absorb that person's behavior patterns.

This means that you will fully imagine yourself in their reality. This is done by using what is known as a second position shift. If you remember from earlier, the second position is what lets you focus on what a person does, which are the things that are the most easily seen. This lets you become aware of how they do things. This is done by adopting their thinking. You will start to figure out why they do the things they do. You will try to find the underlying reasons.

NLP will make use of direct observation to figure out their person's behaviors. This is just like how other modeling methods will try to figure out how to outperform the top performer. They will look at their tonality, words, movements, and so on. This gives you the ability to understand how that person creates their results.

NLP modeling wants you to also understand the why and the how. This will help you to understand what's going on in their head. You will be able to copy them in a more genuine way. The successful performer's why and how can be used to mold your behaviors. This is why the second position is so powerful.

3. Start to produce similar results.

As you begin to act out the person's why and how, you will notice that you will get similar results. Since behaviors could be simple or complex, modeling take a few minutes, hours, days, weeks, months, and possibly years. It will all depend on the complexity of what you are looking to learn.

Since criteria are subjective, find a person that can help you to evaluate whether your results are lining up with the model.

4. Fine tune the pattern.

As you work to perform the behavior or skill, you will start to notice that some things aren't needed. These things aren't needed to produce your desired results. This is where you will fine tune the pattern by testing it to figure what you need to have in it and what you don't. This will also be when you check for improvements.

5. Document the model.

After you have fine-tuned everything, you have to be able to describe the things that are going on. This should be done so that anybody who wants to learn and master this pattern can do so. The easiest way for this to be done is to document the model and then tell an eight-year-old. If they are able to understand what you said, then it's clear.

6. Teach the thing that you have learned.

You become good at something once you can teach it to somebody. You take everything that you have documented and help another person learn the skill. If this ends up being difficult, you will have to modify your description. This should be done until transferring the skill to another becomes easy.

The Right Questions

The most powerful gift that humans have in our communication is the ability to ask questions. Sadly, this is an ability that a lot of people will neglect and is a gift that will often remain undelivered in most communications.

Why would I say that asking questions is a neglected ability? Everybody asks questions. We do, but the art of asking questions is more than making a simple statement and placing a question mark at the end. It's more than a persuasion tactic of some kind to achieve your own objective. It's more than just trying to get your point across, getting your way, or discovering an answer that will benefit you in some way.

We often neglect the art of asking real questions, which is using them as a gift. By gift, I mean asking a person a question without a hidden agenda. Questions that don't have an agenda are questions that you ask a person where you don't have a preconceived objective other than to find out more about what that person thinks. These questions will tell the other that you view them as important. It lets them know that they are more important than you are at that moment.

One of our main motivations in life, other than staying safe, eating, and drinking, is that we want to feel important. Think about the things that are motivating you at this moment? Progressing in your career? Changing your career? Improving your skills? Becoming or feeling successful? Becoming a better parent? The majority of the things that drive us are subconscious needs to feel important.

Through asking a simple question, showing interest, or seeking an opinion, you are sending that other person a message that they are important to you.

The only way this is done is through asking questions during a conversation where you leave behind your values and beliefs. Let's look at it this way.

You're talking with a friend and you ask them a question, "What are your plans this weekend?" This is a seemingly innocent question and it could be completely innocent, however, if you asked the question to try to get your friend to ask a similar question, knowing that you have fun things planned, then these questions come with an agenda. This would be a slight form of manipulation.

You could ask them several questions like "How is your work going?" This is a great starter. Then you ask, "Is your boss still giving you problems?" Using the word still implies that there has been a problem and it could make the other person think that they need to have it fixed. If a question has an implication, then it has an agenda. Do you ask this question to get across your own beliefs? Maybe you believe that problems need to be sorted out fast. Maybe your values are coming through. Frank and open communication are important to you.

Then your next question tells everything, "Shouldn't you get something done about that problem? I would challenge them." This may be a question, but are you actually interested in finding out the answer? These types of questions will likely cause your friend to feel manipulated or criticized. You definitely didn't deliver a gift. You have made yourself feel important.

There are certain ways that you can use language that can imply useful measurements, energy, or lengths of time. The following should be seen as a general guide of those things and what you should look out for when conversing with a person.

- Questions with "Why"

With NLP, we try to avoid starting a question with why. This is because it's hard to predict how much detail somebody could respond with. Why is extremely ambiguous. Every concept, idea, or thing is able to be viewed from different levels of abstraction. This means a person can look at the big picture or fine details. If you are to ask somebody, "Why do you have that job?" they would be able to respond with large concepts like monetary freedom and they skip over the smaller details.

Why also has the tendency to come off as negative. If you ask a person why they aren't able to do something, their brain will go through their resources and memories to pull together the reason why they aren't able to do it. This works like a negative affirmation. It will provide them with a long list of excuses and it won't help them move forward.

- Try using "How"

How questions are more likely to help people think outside their head. Why questions make them look inside themselves, but how will make them look outside themselves to find information that they may not have moved before. How is also infinite in the answers it can create.

Let's assume that in front of you stands a 40-foot wall. Try to come up with five creative ways to get over that wall. How can you do it? Since I first asked you for five ways, you likely came up with five, maybe a few more, and stopped. But think about what happens if I were to just leave you with the how questions.

How could you get over the wall? Think until you run out of ways. How else could you accomplish it? How else? Were you able to squeeze out a couple more?

Now you can see the power of a how question over a why questions.

Asking a good question is an art form and more artists will spend their entire lives perfecting their art. The best way to learn how to ask a question without a hidden agenda is to practice. The next time you are talking with a person, try using some of these tips to leave your agenda at the door:

- Get into a curious mindset. Become really interested in finding out what the other person wants to share.

- Listen closely to their answers. Silence your mind and remove your thoughts that you could experience while they are talking. These are normally opinions forming and you don't want to be interested in your opinions. You are to be interested in theirs.

- Wait for them to answer before you come up with your next question.

- Try asking yourself, "What do I need to understand so that I can understand the whole picture?" Take that answer and form it into a question. What other information do you need? Ask that.

- Try to stay away from questions that use the word why. Why will often lead to the person being asked a question to feel like they have to justify what they did. If you ask, "Why do you go shopping in the morning?" They could interpret it as "Why do you feel like you need to shop?" or "Why would you go in the morning when you could go in the afternoon?"

- Believe in the best of that person. In their own right, everybody is magnificent. What is it that you should ask so that you can let their magnificence shine through?

Now that you have a good idea of how to ask the best question, I want to leave you with two more suggestions. When you can't see to figure out what to ask, try one of these options:

"Is there anything that I've not asked you that you believe would be important or useful to let me know?"

And,

"Is there anything that you want to ask me that I haven't explained to you?"

There will almost always be something that the other person will say to both of these questions because people don't like to have this feeling that there is something that hasn't been answered. It will also take some responsibility and pressure off of you to get all of the information out of the other person.

Personal Beliefs

Our personal beliefs have very little basis in facts but are instead formed from a generalization of what we have experienced, perceptions and views of ourselves, the external world and others, and what we hear from different places that we accept as trustworthy, especially when we were growing up. We will also form beliefs from our own environment and the culture we grew up in. These beliefs will hang around if they stay unproven and will stay with us right through our adulthood. However, there are some beliefs that are based on facts. These would include the law of gravity or other laws about the world.

Beliefs will often control our behavior and they exert a lot of influence on our adversity or otherwise. People act based on their beliefs because they believe them to be true. As long as a person believes that they are unable to do something, their belief will remain an inhibition and they won't ever do it. Even if they do give it a shot, their odds of success are low because they have a negative belief. The reverse is true as well. If a person believes that they are capable of doing something and they do it, they will likely have a successful outcome. This is basically a self-fulfilling prophecy.

Beliefs work like a mental filter. You interpret your external world according to your beliefs. Anything to the contrary won't be accepted because they don't support your beliefs unless it's an exceptional quality. Beliefs will dictate the way that you interact with others. For example, if you were to believe that somebody doesn't like you, you will probably avoid them or try to keep from talking to them. In response, they will likely stay aloof and distant and this will confirm your belief even if they don't actually dislike you.

Over time, your beliefs will change. This is inevitable as you grow and are exposed to more experiences and events. These things will change your beliefs. Not only are your beliefs changed, but it will create empowering ones too. Since beliefs influence behaviors and they create a positive result, you will keep them, otherwise, you will likely change them. Sometimes, you can replace limiting beliefs with suitable ones that will improve your life. When you change your inner limiting beliefs, it will make your behaviors change for the better. This affects your life significantly and can lead to more positive changes. Erroneous beliefs will also have disadvantageous implications. That's why it is important that you replace them with something that is appropriate for you.

The more positive beliefs you have, the more freedom you will have. You will find more possibilities and opportunities. Your success will be improved. Through NLP, you are able to create and choose your own empowering beliefs. That way, you will be able to exploit and develop your potential to reach your desires. However, those belief changes might not last if you allow yourself to give up too soon.

Building Connections

A good use of NLP is being able to establish good communication skills. Leading and pacing is a couple of techniques that you can use to develop rapport. For example, if you live in the United States, you will be able to understand this example better. People who live in different regions will talk at different rates of speed. This is also called pace of speech.

A person living in northern states will always talk faster than somebody from a southern state. This could and sometimes does lead to conflicts and misunderstandings. If you live in a northern state, you can build rapport by slowing down your pace of speech to match a person from a southern state. If you can match their pace, you will make them comfortable around you. This is how to build rapport.

Building trust, harmony, and friendships are the way to make better relationships. These are the main components of building trust and acceptance. Having goodwill toward others can make it easy to open up, connect with other, and having great interactions.

Everyone has a certain type of person who they click with naturally and prefer to interact with. If communication between these two people isn't in sync, it would be safe to say, they aren't going to get along. It might still be easy to create strong relationships or rapport with these people.

After you have learned to pace your speech, you can start using rapport. For example, as you continue talking to this person, you lean back. After some time, they do it too. This is leading.

This sounds manipulative, but if you can use it ethically, it is a great tool to improve rapport. When you can improve rapport, you will improve your communication.

If you can use it correctly, you can convey messages that will resonate to others. It can help build communication and reduce conflicts.

Building Rapport

The following are some techniques that will help you build rapport with others. Some might seem a bit silly but they all work well.

- Mirroring

This is such an easy technique. You do it by mirroring their speech patterns and gestures.

Basically, this is mimicking the behavior of whomever you might be talking to. When talking about the law of attraction, people can bond with others better if they exhibit the same traits. First impressions do last. This is why mirroring is an important technique when you begin interacting with others. Mirroring makes it easier to figure out people's energies and to build rapport.

Let's say you are talking to someone and they cross their arms and lean toward you. To mirror them subtly, start by crossing your hands. Now, tilt your head toward them slightly. If they begin talking loud, you will answer them in a loud voice. Continue mirroring their movements such as if they rub their arm, gently touch yours. Make sure your movements remain subtle. You don't want to rub your arm or deliberately copy everything they do. They might think you are mocking them and get offended.

By mirroring the other person, they will subconsciously see that you are both on the same page. Now, you try to get them to follow your lead.

1. Body Language

   If the person you are speaking with is sitting straight, you need to sit straight. If they cross their arms, cross yours. If they tilt their head, slightly tilt yours. Return gestures such as smiles and handshakes to create trust and courtesy. This will make them feel loved and appreciated and will be more willing to open up to you.

2. Facial Expressions

   We have 53 muscles in our face that can make all sorts of expressions. Everyone can speak volumes without ever saying a work. Are their brows lowered or raised? Are they smooth or furrowed? Is their jaw squared off and tense? Is the bridge of their nose smooth or wrinkled? How fast are they blinking their eyes? A normal person will blink about 15 times each minute. If a person is feeling anxious or is lying, they will blink more. If a person is concentrating, they will blink less. When you match their blink rate, you will have access to their physiological and emotional state. This will take time to master. Since our "eyes are the windows to the soul", it would be worth the effort to try.

3. Breathing Rhythms

   How you breathe tells others the amount of energy you are using. If you are breathing slowly, it shows you are relaxed and calm. Breathing fast shows nervousness or anxiety. Which way do you want others to see you?

4. Match Tempo, Rhythm, and Tone

   The matching voice is a great tool to use if you work in sales or do cold calling. When you work this way, you can't rely on your body language.

   You need to match the other person's tone such as amused, interested, dry, happy, or excited along with the speed at which they are talking. If the other person talks very fast in an excited voice, you need to keep up with them and sound excited too. If they speak carefully and slow, you need to do it too. With practice, this will come naturally.

   Being loud shows intense emotions. It shows signs of frustration and anger. Someone speaking very soft shows they are calm.

   Pitch indicates the tone of voice. A high pitch means excitement while a low one shows anger. It is like an informal but serious conversation such as a person in sales will always use a moderate pitch.

   The rate is how fast you are talking. If your voice gradually increases, it shows you are becoming more intense. Having too many rates shows you are nervous. Disinterest and boredom are also associated with a slow rate.

   Quality is the key to being understood. A person's speech habits, articulation, and pronunciation are things you should remember to communicate effectively. If they talk deliberately and slowly, you need to pace them to match their energy level. When matching their pace, you need to be subtle and natural.

If you are a slow speaker, you might have to quicken your pace to match the other person.

Silence controls how the conversation flows. You need to match your partner's silence. Being silent will give you the chance to regroup your thoughts and listen.

5. Sensory Predicates

   Many people will favor one of the four sensory-based systems that allow us to understand our experiences and world. Basically, it is the words we use to describe these experiences. It is helpful to see keys that show the person's favored system so you can use similar words to have meaningful conversations. Many people will put all the systems into their vocabulary but will favor one over the others. Here are the four systems:

   Auditory: They will use phrases or words like give me your ear, on another note, tune out, tune in, loud and clear, clear as a bell, resonate, listen, tell, hear, and sound.

   Feeling/Kinesthetic: They will use phrases and words like hand in hand, make contact, get in touch with, heated debate, unfeeling, solid, sharp as a tack, concrete, hard, fuzzy, grasp, feel, and touch.

   Visual: They might use phrases and words like hazy, picture this, an eyeful, paint a picture, short-sighted, focused, reveal, bright, clear, foggy, view, look, and see.

   Auditory Digital: They might use phrases and words like conceive, word for word, pay attention to, make sense of, figure it out, learn, motivate, experience, understand, consider, decide, process, learn, know, and think.

Always use caution when you mirror another person. Never look like a robot and don't do everything the other person does. Begin with posture and move on to body language until you have reached the mimicking stage. When the person you are talking with return the favor, make your movements smaller. Rapport is matching energy to the people you interact with.

- Systemic Processes

Everyone's minds are connected to their environment. All the stimuli you get from the world enter our brains to be interpreted. After, our minds will perceive these stimuli as either positive or negative. If you put a negative view on a situation, it is going to remain negative and you will view it as a mistake until you make the effort to find positive things about it. These perceptions will eventually become a reality.

- Filtering

NLP believes that each behavior has a positive intention. This positive intent might not be clear or make sense to everyone. The person who is doing this behavior, it makes total sense in their reality. This can help to explain why everybody doesn't want the same things in life or doesn't react the same way to what happens in life. This shows we all have different perceptions and no one is either right or wrong.

You might not agree with someone else's reality, you can't judge them. You need to respect and appreciate that they have different values and beliefs. Respect that they perceive, feel, see, and hear the world differently. They aren't going to have the same values or make the same choices.

If you are talking with a person and they suddenly raise their voice, yells, and then disappears into their room, you might think this is totally unacceptable. Just be curious. Look at it from their perspective. Their view of the world and their circumstances might cause them to feel overwhelmed or uncomfortable during the conversation and they felt this was their only option.

Filters get developed by things like your family, values, beliefs, spiritual practices, or assumptions while growing up. If you don't like your habits, beliefs, or filters, you are the only one who can change these.

The first thing you must do is to become aware of whether they are detracting or attracting to your life. These are the way you see the world. It drives your behaviors and emotions. This is your reality. It is unique to you. If you would like to get different results out of your reality, NLP can change these beliefs.

- Cause and Effect

Most people live their lives in effect. This means they blame circumstances and others for their bad moods. Other people have to make them feel good about themselves. You might be thinking that "If my spouse only understood me, I'd be happier." Sorry dear, you are the only person who has the ability to change that. Have you told your spouse how you feel? If not, how are they going to know? You might be resisting because you just think they don't care. If you continue on this path, nothing is going to change.

If you would like to be the cause, you are making the decisions and creating what you want out of life. You don't rely on others to be happy and you know that. You can be supportive and cheer others while moving forward. You can't take responsibility for other people's emotional states. If you do this, you are putting a huge weight on your shoulders that will eventually drain you. When using cause, you take responsibility for your actions both bad and good. You realize the world is full of opportunities and you have choices to achieve what you want out of life.

- Respond While Pacing

When pacing, you have to respond instead of reacting to what other people are doing or saying. You react when you make a negative judgment about what others are saying. Don't try to disguise it, it will make them uncomfortable and they could become very aggressive.

Responding is listening to the other person and then reflecting their words back to them. You have to do this without judging. This can help you be sure you understand what the other person is saying. This lets them know you accept what they have said. It doesn't matter if you agree with them or not.

Once you respond, they won't see you as a threat. This lets them relax. They will be less guarded and it will be easier for you to move the conversation where you would like for it to go.

- When to Lead

In order to lead, you have to be sure the other person is in rapport with you. You have to first use mirroring and matching. Then, move your body slightly. Change your tone and see if they follow your lead.

When they do, then you have taken the lead. If not, go back to mirroring and matching.

The main thing is to pace yourself, try to get feedback from their language pattern and body language. When done correctly, mirroring gets them to create a positive image of you.

When you establish rapport, you will be able to lead the way.

- Failing is Great Feedback

Everybody is going to make mistakes and fail. The main thing that separates us is the way we let it affects us either negatively or positively and the way we look at it. With NLP, it is thought that failure doesn't exist, it is all just a feedback. If something doesn't happen the way you think it should, you aren't a failure. It just means you found something that won't work for you. This gives you the opportunity to figure out ways to improve and do better.

Using Your Words and Voice

Language is a powerful tool to help you reach your goals. People that know how to use language skills usually get into positions of power. Especially when talking politics. This involves making a lot of speeches and is connected to persuasiveness. This factor lets you bring others to your viewpoint, interests, and opinions and will subsequently affect their actions. By infusing specific information into phrases, words, or sentences, you can subliminally persuade data and manipulate people. It is easy for our brains to form connections if it has the right conditioning. It can then learn to connect stimulus to reflexes and that could be just one single word. This alone shows how powerful words are. If words are used the right way, it can change a person's opinion about anything by persuasion. They can trigger a person's imagination and could lead to certain thought patterns and affect how well we do specific skills.

Humans have an innate capacity for learning languages. This simply means that when we are exposed to the correct stimulus, we will be a part of the visual-lingual system of recognition. Our brains associate words with specific emotions, meaning, qualities, and objects. We learn to make connections between the given stimulus in the surroundings and a specific work that was provided from the person's native language. Within everyday sentences, there is a level of uncertainty because a sentence might contain phrases or words that suggest meanings other than what the speaker meant. For example look at this sentence: "Flying planes could be dangerous." This might mean that planes when flying are dangerous or flying planes could put you in danger. In certain languages, one word could have several different meanings. In the English language, the word "orange" means a color and fruit. Our brains register every possible meaning for every word or phrase.

These alternate meanings or hidden connotations can be used in many conversations letting a person play the dominant part in all sorts of interactions. In spite of the fact that the brain can recognize which one is the right meaning of the phrase or word. You can use the given situation and environment to find the meaning. It will still register all the possibilities that might apply. Using rapport is a needed part of the whole endeavor along with other factors like tonality and tone of voice that will exhibit the smallest agreement in the person's statements because it lets them relate easier to you. The correct use of body language is also important.

If this uncertainty gets combined with the right body language and gestures to enhance specific meanings, without the listener noticing, the phrase could carry to the unconscious listener a brand new meaning. When making a statement like: "You know whom you can trust in that case" while talking about your subject and while pointing to yourself, you will send a message to the receiver that it is natural for them to trust you even if the original meaning is something completely different.

The main key to achieving persuasion is to get the person to imagine what you want to show them and get them to see the things you want to see. Making some who is close-minded and argumentative to be more flexible, or getting a client to see how good they are going to feel after receiving your company's benefits. The easiest way to do this is as a question using "if-question" like "What would it feel like if you took the option that I am offering you?" What is in question is the actual thing you would like for them to do. This type of question can generate a feeling you would like them to experience or an idea you would like for them to access by triggering their imagination. This is a powerful tool.

Every suggestion, statement, or sentence we hear, could have the ability to create pictures in our emotions and minds. It acts as a trigger for our imagination by picturing the information that we have been exposed to. This, in turn, will generate thoughts based on the information we received. These thoughts will carry the emotion we first generated and it continues until it gives us a conclusion. If the emotion that was transmitted wound up being negative, then the conclusion will be a negative one, too. Because the thought structure that happens from the statement is negative if the listener doesn't reject the statement and the suggestions say so.

If we have reached a certain conclusion about a subject many times, our brain will register that conclusion, as a rule, it will apply to every situation. If a person constantly shows up late for dates, then you will make a conclusion that this person is late always and from that point on, you will expect them to be late and will take measures such as texting them to remind them to be sure they are on time. To flip it around, the person who is getting these messages realizes that they are expected to be late and forms a picture of them being late. This causes them to come to the same conclusions and start believing it and making it come true and this becomes an unconscious rule.

This can also be used to make restrictive rules about a person's abilities. If a person receives a poor grade a couple times in math, they form a belief that they aren't good in math and then this person's skills in math become poor. They will keep this thought from that point on unless they form a new belief that will remove that rule.

Knowledge can also be used to increase a person's skills. If you can understand that there are techniques you can use to control your ability levels, you can change your programming on what you are and aren't good at. You can remove all those negative ruled statements that keep your abilities at bay. You can start putting more effort on specific skills and you will prove that you are good at it and will replace a negative statement with a positive one. Another effective way to improve a specific skill is by using the "power of words". This is using a conditioner to make a trigger for better skill performance. This is similar to what Pavlov did with his dogs. We can train our brains to form connections between a stimulus and being good at a skill of choice.

Words have power because they can influence people indirectly and directly in many different ways. These can be abused and used because they serve to meet a person's interest. It could be a specific weapon, career choice in politics or marketing, or any profession that takes charisma. Linguistic skills are valuable tools that can help you fulfill your goals and help you as a person.

Conflict Resolution

Studies have shown that managers have found themselves in the middle of many conflicts. You might have a different view of the problems or situations than others. You might both believe in different things and it seems like you just aren't going to agree. You might get frustrated since you believe the other person isn't being considerate. You might have teenagers at home that you are always butting heads with. You might even see co-workers who are having a conflict but don't know how to help them. The conflict might sometimes feel like a contact sport. You might be a person who likes to stay away from conflict because you worry about what might happen. This might mean you completely ignore it, let it come to a head, and then sacrifice yourself in the end.

It would be great if you could just take some easy steps and be able to increase your ability to resolve conflicts. Would you like to understand the reason behind the conflict? If you experienced a conflict and you had tips to help you manage it better and are able to move beyond it, wouldn't it be great? Would you like to help others people who are experiencing conflict? How would it feel if you could recognize and take the steps to resolve that conflict before it affects you negatively?

Ignoring conflict is the worst possible thing you could do. A simple definition of conflict is "a disagreement or clash", "a state of disharmony between incompatible interests or ideas", "to be at odds with". If you put your hat into it, it could escalate it from a minor frustration into a monumental problem. You have to deal with it proactively and positively.

What causes conflicts? Many things such as power struggles, jealousy, pride, having a bad day, competitive tensions, and egos can all cause conflicts. Many conflicts are created from two things — emotions and poor communication.

- Poor communication: Is it not having any information, poor information, misinformation, or lack of information? You might have gotten all the information you need in the correct time frame, the problem is you aren't sure how you can process it. Some information might be missing and when you try to add two plus two, you wind up with ten. You add up information, make assumptions, and generalize to make sense of what you have been given. We can probably all relate to this. Remember that communication is more than just words. There is around 55 percent of the communication will be non-verbal. This is body and physiology language. About 38 percent is tonality and seven percent is actual words.

- Emotions: As some may know, emotions can drive the agenda. The challenge is when our emotions take over the driver's seat. If you remember the conflict, you can see where the emotions took over. Were you able to resolve the conflict successfully? Many executives let their emotions take over and lead to irrational thoughts, things getting said that was totally exaggerated, etc. If you have witnessed somebody in a rage, that does or says something that if they weren't enraged would never have said. Emotions that are overindulged during conflict situations don't ever lead to successful outcomes.

Here are some tips on how to resolve conflict:

1. Disassociate yourself from the conflict

You need to put yourself into the position of the observer. This is a place of no emotions. You need to watch yourself with the conflicting party. Take the emotions out of the conflict and you will get more wisdom. Put yourself into the emotions of another and handle the conflict.

2. Disassociate yourself from the person

How hard is it to negotiate when human life is at stake? When the stakes are high for other people, and there might not be a winning situation because of external factors and players but a good outcome is critical. Your feelings or wellbeing might be at stake when you are resolving the conflict for other people. Most people focus on negotiation when human life is an "object." This is so you can negotiate and save as many lives as possible. When preparing yourself for conflict resolution, take a tactical standpoint to help out.

3. Build rapport

We've covered this above but you have to remain calm. You must match the tonality, speed, and volume of the person you are in conflict with WITHOUT mimicking their angry comments.

4. Outcome frame

Having an outcome frame will help focus your thinking and you will be able to find an outcome. You will be able to succeed in resolving conflicts. In many cases, the parties like to cover old ground to lay blame. You need to ask yourself why you want to blame others. Will it get you closer to finding a resolution or the outcome you want? Create an approach that will solve your problem and use the skills you have learned to solve the conflict.

5. Listen actively

If we are completely honest with ourselves, we can all be better listeners. We only listen so we can respond. This means we often miss critical information that others are sharing. Our minds will naturally delete, generalize, and distort information. Remember that conflict is created from emotions and communication. Try to keep your focus on listening or trying to understand something from another.

6. Positive Intention

Many people who are in conflict will drown in details. Many times this is where the true argument stems from. On a high level, what does each part want security, space, love, or respect? Once you can identify this, it helps you create a better strategy to resolve the conflict.

7. Pattern interrupt

Many times during a conflict, it would be best to stop the chain of downward spiraling. This also interrupts the pattern. Make a calm statement such as: "It is important to me that we resolve our problems, but I need to take a moment. I'm going for a walk and will come back and resolve this problem in 20 minutes."

8. Step in somebody else's shoes

You've heard the old saying: "You can't understand somebody until you have walked a mile in their shoes." This still holds true today. Some people have a natural ability to be concerned with the needs of others. If you can put your awareness into somebody else's shoes, it could help you know what they are feeling. You could learn what they hear and see as you talk to them. It gives you an understanding of what they want and needs. Basically, it could help you understand them better. When you can take on the role of a detached person, you will be able to observe the interactions between others. This position encourages you to become impartial. You are basically watching the argument as if it were on the television. Watching the interactions between two people will bring a new perspective to the conflict. This new perspective will not be grounded in the views of either party.

NLP Applications

There are many aspects of your professional and personal life where you can use NLP. Let's look at a few:

Personal Life

Most people feel that there is something keeping them away from success. That "something" is often themselves. The best NLP application is getting control over your life.

Many people don't even know what they want out of life but NLP can change that. Once you find your purpose, it will help you align your values and goals. This covers family, relationships, health, career, and money. Being aligned can help you move toward success fast. It also helps you to get and remain motivated.

Most people hold only pessimistic and negative beliefs about their abilities and themselves. How you think about yourself will affect every single thing you try to do. It can either hinder or help your success. The main problem is many people think habitually.

You can also use NLP to reduce anxiety and stress. There are many powerful and simple techniques that many people have used to get rid of phobias and anxieties. There are other techniques that help you release unwanted behaviors and emotions from the past.

NLP is a powerful tool to improve communication. You can achieve this by developing rapport. This rapport can attract the right people to you. It can also be used to improve your relationships.

Business Life

Processes like leading and pacing can help improve sales. It also improves negotiation skills.

Having better communication skills could help you make stronger partnerships with suppliers, vendors, and customers. It can help you communicate with people who have different backgrounds easily.

These processes can help you understand and analyze the way your team members communicate. This help to create better functioning teams.

You will be a better facilitator and coach. You will have the ability to lead productive meetings. You will soon be the leader people want to look up to. The leader that people would love to follow.

NLP helps you will the hard parts of the business which is the people part.

Conclusion

Thank you for making it through to the end of NLP: The Ultimate Guide to Manipulation, let's hope it was informative and able to provide you with all of the tools you need to achieve your goals whatever they may be.

You've now learned many different NLP techniques. The next thing for you to do is to start using them. Practice makes perfect, and that's what you need to do with NLP. With some time and practice, you will be able to use NLP practices without thinking about it.

Lastly, if you enjoyed this book I ask that you please take the time to review it on Audible.com. Your honest feedback would be greatly appreciated.

Thank you.

Now, I would like to share with you a free sneak peek to another one of my books that I think you will really enjoy. The book is called "Mindfulness Meditation: A Practical Guide for Beginners" Published by Barrie Muesse Scott and Mark Davenport. It's an Introduction to Learn Meditation and Become Mindful Guided Meditation, Self Hypnosis, Subliminal Affirmations, Stress Relief & Relaxation.

Enjoy!

This book is all about using the power of your thoughts to be mindful and bring peace, purpose, and happiness to your life.

Drawing upon the rich tradition of Buddhism, mindfulness

meditation is all about using your thoughts to be present in the moment and crafting the world that you want to live in. If you want to be more present in your daily life, this book is for you. If you want to heal and cope with chronic diseases, this book is for you. If you want to just sleep better or deal with your depression, then this book is definitely for you. Mindfulness meditation has been shown to have extraordinary effects on your life from your mental to physical health. This book will show you how to tap into the beautiful power of mindfulness meditation no matter if you are Buddhist or not.

The following chapters will discuss everything you need to know about embracing mindfulness meditation in your day-to-day life. However, an important distinction between mindfulness and meditation needs to be made before we proceed. Oftentimes, you see mindfulness and meditation used together. Other times, you may see mindfulness and meditations used interchangeably. Meditation is the more general term that refers to the practice of fine-tuning your mind through various mental exercises. Mindfulness is a form of meditation in which one focuses on being in the very moment compared to other types of meditation practices that may use chants or mantras. For the purposes of this book, it is important to note this distinction. Any meditation practice is great! However, this book will dwell on the importance of honing in on your breath with your mindfulness meditation practice.

Mindfulness Meditation: A Practical Guide For Beginners covers five chapters. In chapter 1, mindfulness meditation will be discussed thoroughly. How key concepts in mindfulness meditation relate to Buddhism, plus the benefits of mindfulness meditation, plus answers to frequently asked questions are included. The subject of chapter 2 is about how to practice mindfulness meditation. A practical guide about which positions are best and other best practices are highlighted. Chapter 3 explores more breathing and relaxation techniques that can be used to bolster your mindfulness meditation practice. The techniques in this chapter are able to help you vary your mindfulness meditation practice. Chapter 4 is dedicated to guided mindfulness meditation exercises that can help you as you begin your meditation practice. The scripts included will help you get started so you do not have to start your meditation practice from scratch. Chapter 5 is also dedicated to guided meditations, but the mindfulness meditation scripts in this chapter focus on guided meditations designed to heal various ailments.

This book about Mindfulness and Meditation will more than prepare you to begin your journey into mindfulness and meditation. There are a lot of famous people who practice mindfulness like Naomie Harris, Boris Johnson, Katy Perry, Richard Branson, and Anderson Cooper to name a few; thus, you are in great company.

There are plenty of books on this subject on the market, so thanks again for choosing this one! Every effort was made to ensure it is full of as much useful information as possible. Please enjoy!

Chapter 1: What is Mindfulness Meditation?

> "To think in terms of either pessimism or optimism oversimplifies the truth. The problem is to see reality as it is." – Thích Nhất Hạnh

How many times have we been encouraged to see the cup half full instead of half-empty? Oftentimes in western society, the push to be optimistic and to think positive is drilled into us from a young age. However, if one is beginning to become more mindful, the transition to mindfulness may feel a little jarring as it is opposite of what feels comfortable. Imagine this. Instead of focusing just on the positive aspect of life, mindfulness encourages a realistic outlook on life that embraces the good and the bad, the positive and the negative and the neutral. And this is where our book begins, starting off by learning about this effective way of living that has been used successfully for centuries – mindfulness meditation.

Buddhist monks have been using the power of mindfulness for over 2, 500 years. Mindfulness is the act of allowing your brain to rest while observing the thoughts that come and go in your mind. Mindfulness meditation is different from actively thinking and using your creative mind. When you are being mindful, you focus on an object, scene or sound that is calm and then let your thoughts gently amble by in your mind. Being mindful is powerful because if you are always caught up into being busy and always thinking about your next step, mindfulness gives you a much-needed break and makes you reflect on your pattern of thoughts and actions. It is the exact opposite of the daily living experience of most people because instead of going, mindfulness encourages you to slow down the pace.

Mindfulness allows you to know your thoughts instead of trying to change them. Instead of being judgmental and unkind to yourself if you think something negative, mindfulness has no judgment value on your thoughts. Your thoughts are just there. When you are mindful, you are taking notes of your thoughts like a note-taker. When you are in a mindful state, you just pay attention to what your thoughts are doing but giving them the freedom to do what they want. Ultimately, the goal of mindfulness is to know your mind. Once you begin to know your mind, you can begin the next step which is to train your mind.

The beautiful thing about our minds is that they are malleable, and as a result, they are trainable. Our minds are able to change based on what one is thinking. If you think the world is a horrible place, you will operate from a place of fear and your actions will show that. If you think that the world is a wonderful place, you will operate from a place of reckless optimism without being able to be realistic about certain dangers you may find yourself in. Mindfulness helps you to know your thoughts and then begin to train your thoughts to become more in tune with your long-term goals. Mindfulness slows down the grind of your busy daily pace and gives you a different vantage point about patterns in your life. These patterns can be feelings that you have in certain situations or your reactions to how other people treat you. When you are being mindful, you may notice trends and patterns that you are constantly thinking. Are you always wanting more and more? Do you feel comfortable with the way things are? Whatever patterns you notice, mindfulness can help you pinpoint what types of things are causing you mental, anguish, conflict, or joy. Then after noticing these patterns, you can begin to shape it to how you would like to be by focusing on being more gracious, compassionate, and kind with your thoughts.

When you begin your practice, do not treat your mindfulness meditation practices as an obligatory item on your daily to-do list. When you meditate, you want to be present in the moment, not treating the practice as an aggressive measuring stick to how fast you can change or using your meditation practice as a form of escapism without being willing to change your ideals. The most important thing to remember before you begin is that you are training your mind to be at peace with how things are going in the world, no matter what is happening. Once you are able to be at peace in no matter what situation you find yourself in, then you are able to start to work on yourself to change your values. Mindfulness meditation is not a sprint; it is a marathon that you continually work on until you are finally able to free yourself from unsavory emotions that are clinging to you whether they are anger, agitation, negativity, self-image issues, unfair, hasty judgments, and biased opinions and ideals.

When you are training your mind to be more mindful, affirmations are great tools to use. Affirmations are very helpful, especially when you create them yourself. The thought process behind using affirmations is to use very direct language which influences your subconscious to help you get the outcome that you want to get. When you use affirmations, you want to first figure out what outcome it is that you want. Then create a short sentence with an active word. Make sure the sentence is in the present tense. For example, if you want to feel calmer and not be so anxiety-ridden, you can create an affirmation to help. You will start with the outcome of being calmer and make that into a statement using the present tense. Thus, the affirmation would be 'I am more calm.' By using the present tense, you are affirming the future outcome. When the affirmation is created, you can say it during your meditation time and throughout the day. When you couple this practice of saying affirmations with your mindfulness meditation session, they work doubly together to help you get the outcome that you want to get. For example, you hear the term think positive all the time. It is because positive thinking can help shape your future to where you have a positive future. However, if you think negative oftentimes a reality reflects your thoughts. Our thoughts influence our subconscious which in turn can determine our reality.

Mindfulness meditation helps you shape your reality by taking the time to know your mind. Once you know your mind, you will be able to train it and ultimately free it from negative, debilitating thinking. Every step works together. Before you begin your mindfulness meditation practice, know that it is not going to be easy. It will be a journey, but if you are dedicated, you will see a difference in your life.

The History of Mindfulness Meditation

For Buddhists, nurturing mindfulness is the ultimate path to enlightenment. The point of Buddhism is to reach the highest truth by focusing on overcoming the limitations that your body has. Buddhists practice mindfulness by using four foundational truths of mindfulness. The four truths originate from a Buddhist sutta or sutra which is similar to a form of Buddhist scripture. The name of the sutta is called "The Discourse on the Establishing of Mindfulness" or the *Satipatthana sutta*. Please remember that the four establishments of mindfulness come from a very long and rich history. This book cannot possibly cover everything related to them, but hopes to serve as a general overview that can deepen your understanding of mindfulness meditation. The four truths are mindfulness of the body, mindfulness of feelings, mindfulness of consciousness and mindfulness of phenomena. Each foundation normally goes step-by-step in a flowing manner. You can go in and out of meditating upon each truth. They all work together. The first stop on the mindfulness journey is mindfulness of the body.

What is the one thing that you typically hear before beginning any form of meditation? The answer is watching your breath. Most meditation practices or guided meditations instruct you to begin by taking deep breaths in and exhaling deep breaths. Therefore, when you practice mindfulness, the first step is to think about mindfulness of your body. Initially, you'll want to start by being mindful of your breathing. Notice how deep or how shorts your breaths are when you start your meditation session. There are also different forms of body mindfulness you can focus on as well, such as mindfulness of eating or mindfulness of how you walk. These are some of the easiest mindfulness of the body to begin with, but we will focus on mindfulness of breathing since breathing is key to healing lots of ailments, physical and mental in your body.

Mindfulness of the body is just not about the positions your body is sitting in or how you breathe, eat and walk. Mindfulness of the body also involves a deeper understanding of how all your body parts work together. This includes how your leg connects to your thigh, how your ears function, or the power of body working throughout your body. Mindfulness of the body also seeks to understand some of the more unpleasant bodily functions such as urine or snot boogers or blood. The purpose of being mindful of your body is to reflect on how your body functions. You may ask, how do I try to be mindful of my body when I am meditating? An easy introductory way to do this is to imagine yourself greeting and thanking each body part for what it does. You can start at your feet and work your way up until you reach the top of your body.

The next foundation you should be concerned with when practicing mindfulness meditation is mindfulness of your feelings. A better way to explain mindfulness of your feelings is that this truth is concerned about being mindful of your neutral, painful, and pleasurable feelings. You can also reflect on how to be mindful of these feelings by using the senses of your touch, smell, hearing, seeing, taste, and your mind. In Buddhism, your mind is considered a sixth sense. It important to be mindful of these feelings because when you have painful feelings they can lead to fear and hatred. Too many neutral feelings can cause you to become disinterested and floated through life. When you are neutral about something, you are not concerned about it and as a result, it will not be important to you. Lastly, you have to be mindful of pleasurable feelings because too many pleasurable feelings can lead to lust and greed. It is important to be non-judgmental and only observe your thoughts, not acknowledge them when you meditate. The reason you do not want to acknowledge anything is that once you begin to acknowledge a thought as a neutral, painful or pleasurable feeling, you are in danger of attaching yourself to feelings that will prevent you from being enlightened. Thus, it is best to use mindfulness to observe when you are gaining feelings of neutrality, pleasure or painful so you know how to handle those feelings appropriately. When you practice mindfulness of feelings, you will still experience feelings.

Mindfulness of feelings does not mean that you do not feel. It only means that you are able to enjoy the feelings without going overboard to the point of the feelings cause you to become obsessed and overly attached to the thing that is causing the feeling, whether those feelings are good or bad. For example, if you love doughnuts and you find yourself obsessing over doughnuts, you can enjoy them so much that you want more and more doughnuts because of the pleasurable feeling that doughnuts give you. Eating too many doughnuts can cause issues your health like diabetes or chronic inflammation. All of these feelings started because of the seemingly innocent, yet pleasurable feeling of liking doughnuts. On the other side, if you are leery of a certain political leaning and it brings you immense pleasure, attaching yourself to that displeasure can quickly lead to hatred and biased feelings. However, if you are able to know your thoughts and know that this political leaning causes displeasure, you can work to be mindful that the political leaning is a trigger for you without attaching too much to that feeling to the point that it goes overboard. Likewise, if you feel neutral about a person, you can become so disinterested in them that you lose focus of the fact that they are human and worthy of respect. Hence, if they ever needed something, you would most likely overlook them or drag your feet to help them. So even feelings of neutrality can be dangerous. Once you become too attached to any type of feeling, the excess doting on the feeling prevents you from reaching enlightenment.

The next foundation of mindfulness meditation that you want to build upon is mindfulness of your consciousness. In Buddhism, there are 52 mental formations. Mental formations translated loosely are emotions and states of mind. The mental formations are normally grouped together in a specific way. The first of these formations are the previous feelings that were discussed in the mindfulness of feelings consisting of feelings of pleasure, neutrality, and displeasure. The next 51 formations are what the mindfulness of the consciousness helps you to focus on that are clustered in different groups. These include:

- Proficiency of mental properties
- Pliancy of mental properties
- Perception
- Composure of mind
- Appreciation
- Effort
- Righteousness of mind
- Worry
- Desire to do
- Amity
- Psychic life
- Error
- Perplexity
- Feeling
- Right livelihood
- Volition
- Initial application
- Attention
- Greed
- Buoyancy of mental properties
- Adaptability of mind
- Recklessness
- Right speech
- Sloth
- Discretion
- Proficiency of mind
- Modesty
- Conceit
- Right action
- Faith
- Buoyancy of mind

- Pliancy of mind
- Contact
- Deciding
- Concentration of mind
- Torpor
- Mindfulness
- Disinterestedness
- Envy
- Shamelessness
- Adaptability of mental properties
- Distraction
- Composure of mental properties
- Dullness
- Balance of mind
- Sustained application
- Pity
- Selfishness
- Reason
- Righteousness of mental properties
- Hate

This is a general overview of the mental formations, but you can study them in more detail to get a more detailed understanding. To simplify this foundation, when you are practicing mindfulness of the conscience, be observant of the different feelings that go in and out of your brain. To easily start meditating with mindfulness of the conscience, when you meditate observe any thoughts that you have. When your mind drifts from focusing on your breathing, you can call out to yourself that you are being mindful. When your mind begins to drift from not meditating, you can call out to yourself that you are not being mindful. This simple exercise is using mindful of your consciousness. It is also a great trick to use in your everyday life when you want to be more mindful.

The last foundation of mindfulness that you want to build upon is mindfulness of phenomena or mindfulness of perception. When you think of a car, you know it is an object that has four wheels and has the capacity to take you here and there. The idea that you have in your mind of a car may be realistic and based on a car that you know personally. Or the idea of a car that you may have can be based on what your perception of what a car is generally, according to your knowledge of what a car is. When you practice mindfulness of mental objects, you try to focus on the 'why' of how you perceive something. If you think of cars as positive, this positive association could be because of a childhood memory that when growing up you had a wonderful experience of your parents taking you to school every day in an old beat up, yet comfortable car. If you have a negative perception of cars, it could be because your friend was killed by a car or cars cause you to think of all the damage that they do to the ozone layer. Mindfulness of perception allows you to focus on the experiences that shape your perception of what something is so you can bypass those perceptions to get to the true meaning of what something actually is and not what you think something is.

When you practice mindfulness of perception, you want to be aware of things that can cause your perception to be tainted. These can be known as the 5 hindrances. You also want to be mindful of the 7 factors of awakening which should be what you aspire your perceptions to be based on. When all of these factors work together, it helps you eliminate suffering. The 7 factors of awakening that you want to focus on when you practice mindfulness of perception include:

- Equanimity – This factor can be described as the calm observance of things around you.
- Energy – This is the energy that powers you to lead the investigation to seek understanding about different topics in life.

- Concentration – The complete focus of the mind is what this factor seeks.
- Investigation of your perception – This factor encourages you to seek knowledge about phenomena to understand how something operates.
- Joy – Balanced pleasurable interest in something is what this factor is all about.
- Tranquility – Serenity and quietness encompass this factor.
- Mindfulness – Present moment awareness describes this factor.

The 5 hindrances to avoid are:
- Dullness – Doing your takes half-heartedly with no vim or lacking concentration.
- Lust – A craving for pleasure to fulfill all your senses.
- Ill will – Feelings of hatred directed to others.
- Restlessness and worry – This is when you are unable to calm your mind.
- Doubt – A lack of trust or conviction.

When you monitor your thoughts to see if any of the 5 hindrances appear in your train of thoughts, you want to note when and why they arose. You'll also want to note how you can prevent the hindrance from appearing again and how you can replace the hindrance with one of the 7 factors of awakening in their wake.

As you work on your mindfulness meditation, strive to attain the four foundational truths in the order of mindfulness of body, mindfulness of feelings, mindfulness of consciousness, and mindfulness of perception. This is ideal. However, you can meditate upon all of the foundations in one setting as well. So, if you focus on more than one truth at a time, that is ok as well.

To truly attain enlightenment, you must find a way to master them all.

Lastly, mindfulness meditation helps you cultivate awareness of the "three characteristics of experience." According to Buddhism, if you do not understand these three characteristics, then you are bound to be caught up into an endless cycle of suffering. The three characteristics you should be aware of are the traits of impermanence, or *anitya*, dissatisfaction, or *duhkha*, and egolessness, or *anatma*. Impermanence means that all conditioned things will change. There is a constant change that you must be aware of. The next trait of dissatisfaction means that there is pain and suffering and no satisfaction in an unenlightened state. *Anatma* means that one should strive to act without an ego. These three are another aspect of Buddhist underpinnings behind the mindfulness meditation practice. These are great to keep in the back up your mind when you are doing mindfulness meditation.

Hopefully, up until this point, the case for why you practice mindfulness has been made. In case you still are not convinced, let's try to convince you one more time. So why mindfulness? There are lots of different meditation practices you can choose from, but mindfulness meditation is a great way to begin for a few different reasons.

Mindfulness is awesome because it:
- Helps you not be judgmental – One of the major components of mindfulness is to not be judgmental of yourself and others. This gentleness towards yourself improves your overall self-esteem. It also encourages self-compassion for yourself and for others.
- Easy and fast – There is no set time to do it. It is super easy to pick up on and relatively fast to do. Your

sessions can be as long as they need to be or as short as they can be. If you have a busy schedule, you can meditate for 5 minutes or however long is best for you.
- Reduces stress instantly -Because the necessity of breathing is at the core of mindfulness meditation, deep breathing immediately reduces the stress you may be feeling as soon as you begin your mindfulness meditation session.
- Improves your wisdom – Mindfulness meditation improves your wisdom because you are able to figure out what makes you tick by noting and understanding the power of your thoughts. You also are able to be wise about other people, because this system meditation improves your observation skills such that you will be able to observe others and make connections about their behavior in ways that you have not been able to before.
- No set way to do it – For some people, the fact there is no set structure may be limiting to them, but it is a positive because there is not a right or wrong way to do it.
- Relaxing and calms your nerves – Just like reducing your stress instantly, mindfulness meditation also relaxes and calms your nerves due to the power of breathing.
- Observe yourself in the moment – Mindfulness meditation allows you to be in tune with your thoughts and actions so you are able to get into the 'zone' a lot easier than before.
- Easy to pick-up – Did I mention how easy mindfulness meditation is to pick up? Once you have one session, you will be able to do more rather easily.
- Doesn't have to depend on anyone else to do it – Mindfulness meditation is great to practice on your own. So you never have to worry about if the teacher is going

to show up to class or not. This meditation style is self-guided so you can set your schedule according to your convenience.

Thank you, this preview is now over.

I hope you enjoyed this preview of my book Mindfulness Meditation: A Practical Guide for Beginners - An Introduction to: Guided Meditation, Self Hypnosis, Subliminal Affirmations, Stress Relief & Relaxation. Learn to Meditate and Become Mindful" by Barrie Muesse Scott and Mark Davenport. Please make sure to check out the full book on Amazon.com

DARK PSYCHOLOGY:
PROVEN MANIPULATION TECHNIQUES TO INFLUENCE HUMAN PSYCHOLOGY

Discover Secret Methods for Mind Control, Dark NLP, Deception, Subliminal Persuasion, and Dark Hypnosis

Congratulations on purchasing Manipulation Techniques to Influence People: Dark Psychology 202, and thank you for doing so!

The following chapters will discuss about Persuasion Methods: Analyze People, Mind Control 101, Dark NLP, Dark CBT, Deception, Brainwashing Hypnotism and many more topics. The information found in this book will best explore the methods and techniques you need to learn in order to successfully master Manipulation and be able to Influence People.

Thanks again for choosing this book! Every effort was made to ensure it is full of as much useful information as possible. Please enjoy!

Table of Contents

Chapter 1: Introduction to Dark Psychology 120
    Persuasion 126
    Manipulation 127
    Deception.. 128
    Subliminal Messages 129
    NLP – Neuro-Linguistic Programming 132

Chapter 2: Body Language and Lies 135
    Body Language 135
    Deception.. 140
    The Deception Spectrum 142
    Deceptive Topics 143
    Deceptive Tactics 146

Chapter 3: NLP 151
    NLP: A Brief History 158
    The Pillars Of Nlp: How To Apply The Knowledge In This Guide 160
    NLP Presuppositions 161

Chapter 4: Psychology Of Influence, Persuasion And Manipulation 178

Chapter 5: Brainwash and Hypnotism 190
    Hypnotism Is Real 190
    Hypnotic Tactics 191
    Brainwashing 200
    Brainwashing Contexts 202
    The Process Of Brainwashing 205
    The Impact Of Brainwashing 209

Conclusion 212

Chapter 1: Introduction to Dark Psychology

It's a bit of a well-kept secret that the ability to manipulate people is a useful tool. It's one of the reasons how businessmen and politicians get and hold their positions. There comes a certain point in your life wherein completely turning off your emotions and being pragmatic is a skill you need to have. Nobody likes to discuss it because we have this societal fear of the reality that people can just be seen as a means to an end.

The late Steve Jobs was particularly renowned for his ability to work people's emotions and to say just the right thing that would get them to come around to his view. It was so strong, in fact, that the people around him developed their own term for it: the 'reality distortion field,' a phrase coined from a similar phenomenon in the Star Trek universe.

There are numerous historical instances of Steve Jobs taking advantage of his unique ability to get precisely what he wanted. One such instance was when Jobs, in the 1980s, was trying to get Pepsi CEO John Sculley to come to Apple. This exchange spawned a famous line that many know today: "Do you want to sell sugared water for the rest of your life, or do you want to come with me and change the world?"

There is a lot that can be said about his specific ability to charm and manipulate people, not the least of which was his deep understanding of what people wanted as well as what people wanted to hear. Add on to this an understanding of subtle intimidation, power cues, and a large amount of passion and charisma, and you have a powerhouse who could get pretty much whatever he wanted.

How does all of this apply to you? Well, you're reading this because you want to learn how to work with people from the inside out. You want to know how to say just the right thing to get what you need and how to manipulate people such that you can bypass any obstacles, so they will do exactly what you want. If that's the case, then you've come to the right place.

The fact is that the mind is a relatively simple thing. While the brain is infinitely complex, the manifestations of the conscious mind are both resolute and easy to work with. Most people work in very obvious and predictable ways such that if they're a 'normal' person, you can rather easily figure out the best way to work with them in no time flat.

The purpose is to analyze all of these patterns within the context of people in general so that you can learn the best way to put these trends to use. Some people will, of course, break these 'standard' molds, and for this reason there are a couple chapters dedicated to the idea of knowing the person you're working with, reading their inner and outer body language and mental cues, and knowing how to build a paradigm that you can easily manipulate them with.

In the end, this is about using the concept of neuro-linguistic programming to its fullest to get what you want out of people. A more common term for this is 'manipulation.' However, the aim of neuro-linguistic programming is slightly different. Neuro-linguistic programming is more focused on the long-term shifting of attitudes where manipulation is more based on immediate gains. That isn't to say that neuro-linguistic programming isn't a form of manipulation though, it absolutely is.
When you hear the term 'manipulation,' you will probably have some sort of knee-jerk reaction like, "Wait, isn't manipulation

wrong?" And to this question, there is no simple answer.

I have to say no, though. Manipulation isn't wrong, manipulation is simply a tool. How you use it can determine whether it's wrong or not. For example, an example of manipulation being objectively wrong is doing something that gets somebody terribly hurt. There are also some unspoken rules that you should never break. For example, while it's pretty easy to take advantage of the fact that somebody's parent is dying, actually doing so is a major ethical gray area.

If you stick to maintaining an ethical approach, then manipulation actually proves itself as a method of understanding people and knowing how to work with them so things will work out better for you. You can even use manipulation for good purposes. One such example is Steve Jobs yet again, who used his reality distortion field for good causes, such as when he would convince his employees that it was possible to do something that was more or less impossible, which in turn, would make them work harder for the end result and eventually lead to a new mark being set in technology.

We all know that psychology is the study and analysis of the human mind and human behavior. So, what is Dark Psychology? It is the science and art of manipulating and controlling the human mind through various methods. Psychology is central to human interactions, thoughts, and actions whereas Dark Psychology involves the use of tactics of persuasion, motivation, coercion, and manipulation to get what you want.

There is a phenomenon in this realm referred to as the Dark Psychology Triad that consists of elements that help in detecting potential criminal behavior in people. The Dark Triad is a combination of traits including Narcissism, Machiavellianism, and Psychopathy. What are the characteristic features of each of these Dark Triad traits?

- Narcissism – is related to lack of empathy, high levels of egotism, and grandiosity

- Machiavellianism – People with this attitude have little or no sense of morality and ruthlessly employ manipulation and other tactics to exploit and/or deceive others.

- Psychopathy – These people come across as very charming and charismatic and deep down are highly impulsive, selfish, lack empathy, and are fairly remorseless.

Yes, it is true that none of us wants to be manipulated and yet it happens in our daily lives with unerring regularity, many times unwittingly. Additionally, we also use mind control and manipulation tactics to try and get what we want. Dark Psychology involves studying the psychodynamics of people who prey on and victimize others to achieve their own ends.

There are people who use dark psychology tactics knowingly and with the intention to cause harm to others and there are those who use or are prey to these tactics in unwitting ways. Moreover, it is a survival instinct in all living beings to be wary of our surroundings and use guile and deception to survive and thrive. There are multiple studies that prove this innate ability to victimize others.

Although we believe that we have control over our actions and reactions, under extreme pressure, it is very difficult to predict our behaviors and there are high chances that many employ dark tactics to escape from these pressures. The following studies are examples of how human minds behave in unpredictable ways when compelled or sometimes even when it may not have needed such an extreme reaction.

Let us look at some of these experiments conducted in the '60s and '70s by psychologists. While there are controversies surrounding the experiments and plausible rationalizations were provided in retrospect, it goes without doubt that the human mind can be very unpredictable and is capable of reaching out to its dark aspects with little or no provocation.

The 'learner' was actually only an actor.

If the learner gave a wrong answer, the volunteers were told to give electric shocks by turning the 'dial', which had labels ranging from mild pain to extreme pain to even fatal. The experimenter wearing a lab coat told the volunteers that they should continue to increase the intensity of the 'electric shock' until the right answer was given by the learner. The volunteers could hear the simulated screams of the learner from the other room. If the volunteer did not want to increase the intensity, then the experiment told them to continue employing the following statements:

- Please continue

- The experiment needs you to go on

- It is essential that you go on

- You have no choice; you have to go on

There were startling and disturbing outcomes from this rather controversial experiment. Despite hearing the simulated screams of extreme pain from the 'learners,' 65% of the volunteers turned the knob to 'fatal.' They did not even bother to ask about the health of the learner. Yet, most of the volunteers said that they would have never behaved this way but did not find the wherewithal to stand up to a figure of authority (lab-coated experimenter). Dark Psychology is easy to trigger, isn't it?

The most disturbing observation of these kinds of experiments was the fact that the volunteers were not even aware that they were being manipulated and that they were delving into the dark aspects of their minds. Another study which proved the unconscious behavior under authority goes as follows:

A group of volunteers was asked to watch a screen in which a basketball game was going on. They were told to count the number of passes that took place between players wearing white shirts. At some point during the game, a person dressed in a gorilla costume walked into the court. The participants were so engrossed in counting the number of passes that they did not even notice this aberration. In fact, many participants swore that no such disturbance took place! They were unconsciously following the orders of the experimenter.

Another common dark psychology tactic is called 'priming' in which people's behaviors can be changed without them even realizing it. For example, read this sentence, 'The house was so old that it groaned, creaked, and struggled to stand on its shaky foundation.' Now, suppose you were to stand up, chances are very high that you will unconsciously have taken care to do so at a slower pace than usual as you were just now 'primed' for old age.
Politicians are known to use priming to change voting preferences based on the location of the booth. Like this, there

are many studies which prove that accessing and employing the dark side of our minds is not just easy but can happen without us even being aware of it.

Moreover, these theories have been applied and checked repeatedly throughout the history of mankind and dark psychology is an integral part of our minds. This is not the same as conspiracy theories. Dark psychology only represents the innate need and desire for man to dominate over others who are weaker than himself so as to achieve his own ends. Marketing advertisements are classic examples of manipulating the minds of the buyers and convincing them to buy the product, which they may or may not need.

Therefore, it makes sense to know, understand, and appreciate this aspect of our minds and use strategies and tips to 'prime' our minds and those of others in ways that will result in win-win situations for all concerned stakeholders.

Persuasion

Persuasion is one of the most popular forms of mind control. This method is used in so many different areas of life that many people don't even recognize when it is happening. That is exactly why it works.

Persuasion is not the same as convincing, although most people believe the two are the same thing. However, persuasion is the act of skillfully encouraging someone to do what you want them to do without them realizing you're doing it, whereas convincing someone means that you are using tactics that are easy to recognize. To explain it a bit further, persuading means to skillfully present facts and information in a way that doesn't make it obvious that you are doing so, and encouraging people to do what you desire for them to do.

Convincing people, on the other hand, is very obvious and often includes a lot of back-and-forth and ultimately nagging, begging, or pleading someone to make the decision you want them to make after they have already chosen the alternative.

When you are learning about persuasion, it may seem easy. In reality, it is a strategy that requires a lot of time, effort, and practice. You cannot simply read about persuasion and then run out and master it. Instead, you really need to ensure that you grasp the concept and that you practice putting it into action in your daily life. In chapter 6 you will learn about many real-life strategies that can help you further integrate this technique into your life.

Manipulation

Manipulation tends to be regarded as one of the darker methods of mind control, and many people think it is a nasty thing to do. However, when you learn to use manipulation properly, you can use it to gain control over virtually anyone's mind and have your desired effect on their decisions and actions.

Unlike persuasion, which is typically comprised of conversational tactics, manipulation involves external influences to help encourage people to do what you want them to do. These include strategies like building trust, and proving why they should do what you want them to do. While some of these strategies are conversational, they are often impacted by external influences unlike persuasion which relies merely on wording structure and methods of structuring your sentences and conversations.

Deception

Deception is an extremely sophisticated strategy that is used in mind control. This is not the process of outright lying to people, but rather tactfully covering up certain pieces of information to avoid them from ever being discovered. This strategy allows people to knowingly omit information from conversations without being considered liars since they have never directly been asked, and therefore they have never directly lied.

When you are partaking in deception, you have to be tactful and consistent in keeping the conversation away from any question that may put you in a position where you must either come clean or actually lie. Using deception as a secondary manipulation method for mind control purposes means controlling the conversation and preventing it from ever going in the direction that would suggest information that you are lying or covering up information.

In order to skillfully use deception, you need to know how to guide the conversation in a way that leads the listener to believe something without ever actually being told to believe it. For example, if you want to prevent someone from finding out that you are attracted to someone they also like, you could create the illusion that you are not. You never actually admit that you aren't, you just lead the conversation so that it can be assumed that you aren't.

This is a powerful form of mind control because it allows you to deny ever doing anything wrong. Since you have never admitted to anything or lied about anything, you can easily say that it was the listeners fault for not asking, or for assuming anything was implied.

Subliminal Messages

When you use subliminal messages, you are sending messages without someone actually knowing that you are doing so. These messages tend to slip past the conscious mind and directly into the subconscious. The powerful thing about subliminal messages is that you can be telling someone one thing, and yet having them hear something entirely different. While this conscious mind digests something that they are willingly accepting, their subconscious mind may be hearing something entirely different. Because you have put them into a receptive mode, they are more likely to react and respond in the way that you want them to, and their subconscious mind is more likely to accept the information as well.

Subliminal messaging is powerful because it allows you to control the mind without any indication that you are doing so. You can speak directly through the conscious mind and into the subconscious mind, thus planting information, evidence, and knowledge into the subconscious that encourages your listener to support your position and act or think in the way that you want them to. You are literally programming their mind with your desired messages, and they have no idea that you are doing so.

Mind control is a very powerful strategy that can enable you to have people thinking in your favor. These individuals are going to unknowingly be listening extremely closely to your sentences and hanging on your every word, while giving into anything you want. Because of your masterful ability to control their minds without them even knowing it, you will be able to have any desired outcome effortlessly.

People often have a few different traits which you can use to understand them. Things such as their body language, their life situation, and their emotions. All of these impact one another. In the following chapters, we will break down all of these aspects to help you understand exactly what position you're in.

Body language is a huge giveaway about what's going on in a person's head. Understand that in terms of neuro-linguistic programming, body language is a language in and of itself.

We're going to expand on this concept just a bit so we can gain an understanding of how we can read and process other people's emotions.

This is actually a very critical part of neuro-linguistic programming, and one of the things that makes it such a challenge. Doing it properly is not like picking a lock. There is no 'correct' path for you to do it right. It's a very dynamic activity, which is heavily centered on your ability to understand what the other person is thinking in a very concrete manner.

Understand that a person has many physical tells, but that's not the be-all-end-all of what is going on in a person's mind. Some people are so good at hiding their emotions that you can't really tell what's going on under the hood unless you know them very well.

Often, people will have two emotions running in parallel. These can be difficult to decipher, but generally, they have the emotion at their foreground — this is what they display themselves to be feeling — and they have their emotion in the background, which is what they are feeling under the hood.

Some people are worse than others when it comes to hiding their emotions while some people make no effort at all. There are times, too, where these emotions may run in tandem and are exactly the same.

The truth is, though, that if you're trying to convince somebody of something, you always have to consider the possibility that people don't often feel what they're projecting themselves to be feeling. Usually, you have to consider what these parallel emotions could be.

We'll focus more on the underlying emotions when we get to the chapter on psychoanalysis. However, for now, we just need to focus primarily on reading emotions on the surface.

People convey a lot of their emotions through their body language as well as through their tone of voice and their choice of words.

If you pay attention to a person's eyes, you can read a lot into somebody's foreground emotion. While, hopefully, you're emotionally competent enough to read foreground emotions relatively well, note that some of these can be difficult to break apart from one another. For example, while the difference between annoyance and anger are slight in terms of their physical display, they have far different emotional connotations. Annoyance is much shorter and less severe, though perhaps more immediately snappy. Anger is more brooding and harder to work your way out of.

Their tone of voice will also tell you a lot. Often, when people aren't being completely honest about the emotion they're presenting, their voice will sound ever so slightly off. Being able to recognize this and using context clues to figure out what's really bothering them or going on in their head is very important.

Sometimes their choice of words will give you hints as well. Pay attention and try to notice if their sentences are structured differently. Are they shorter? Is their choice of words more serious than usual?

In essence, pay attention to a person's body language, as it will tell you a lot about what you need to know when it comes to what a person is feeling, at least on the surface level. When you combine that with your analysis of their underlying conditions, you actually get a very potent piece of information that you can work with.

NLP – Neuro-Linguistic Programming

NLP involves the three most powerful elements that contribute to the human experience and they are; neurology, language, and programming. So, how can we use NLP to influence people? Here are some answers to that.

NLP techniques are in use both in businesses and personal relationships to influence people around you. NLP techniques are designed to help you get your message across in the correct way so that they are interpreted by the people to give you your desired outcomes. NLP techniques also focus on the choice and appropriate use of language to help you motivate people around you to get something good done.

NLP techniques are designed in such a way that if used correctly, they can help you teach others how to become more productive and efficient in their lives which, in turn, helps you in your life as well. NLP techniques are also designed for salespeople so that they are able to reach the subconscious levels of the buyers' minds in such a way that they feel good and happy about buying the product or service.

The basic presumption of NLP is that each of us is unique in the way we think, we interpret, and the way we present ourselves to the outside world. NLP says that if we know how we think, then we can be empowered to change the way we think. Extending the same logic outside of us, if we know how people think, we can empower ourselves and them to influence changes in their thought processes.

Let us take an example. Each of us has a unique way of translating what we see around us into thoughts. Our preference could be to the use of sight, sound or touch or a unique combination of all three. If our preferred sense is that of sight, then we easily convert the events in our life into pictures and images in our thoughts. If our preferred sense is that of touch, we easily convert our experiences into feelings.

Let's take this a bit further. Suppose you had a preference for the sense of sight. This preferred sense is actually very evident in the way you interact with others. For example, you will use phrases like, 'See you later,' or 'I can see how this will turn out,' etc. You will normally be the type of person who decides that when something or someone is out of sight, then that person or thing is out of your mind too.

So, with a person whose sense preference is that of touch, phrases such as 'Catch you later,' or 'I'm getting a bad feeling from this,' etc. will be used. So, by knowing these preferences and the way they become evident through their language and thought, we can understand people better and once we understand their behavior, we can more easily influence the way they think.

It is a natural thing to be fond of those individuals who are like us in the way they think and behave. So, by knowing their preferred means of communication, we can use the same way to communicate with them and therefore make it easy for us to influence them.

A classic example of NLP influencing technique is to synchronize your breathing with that of the other person. Watch when the person breathes in and you match your inhalation with that. When you match every breath of yours with the other person's, you will find an invisible connection to the individual giving you a great boost in terms of influencing his or her thoughts.

Chapter 2: Body Language and Lies

Body Language

Humans are adept at reading body language or the nonverbal signals we use to communicate. These nonverbal cues can communicate more information that the words we choose. From facial expressions to how we stand, the things we don't say convey volumes of information.

People have a natural inclination to engage in helping behavior. Our communal nature makes it imperative to understand the meaning behind nonverbal cues. This makes every person on earth a mind reader. It just so happens that some people are better at it than others.

Our communities aren't a big homogenous mass though. We divide up into micro and macro groups and prioritize our "tribe" when making decisions. In the long run, it provides significant benefits to team up rather than every person for themselves.

But our mind-reading abilities add a layer of complexity. Humans can lie or otherwise hide their true intentions. This often provides a significant short-term advantage at the cost of ill will from others in the community.

Deception is an active performance. It requires decent brain power and effort to maintain a ruse for any length of time. We can only focus on a few things at a time so our body language often gives away our true thoughts and intentions.

I have learned a few tricks that can help anyone improve their ability to influence others through body language. They are simple but have helped everyone from vacuum salesmen to Ted Bundy hide their true intentions.

These techniques aren't going to stop racism, misogyny or ass-hats. But they can pressure others to respond in subtle or overt ways. With enough practice and proper execution, they will push people over the fence of suspicion and help you change a no into a yes.

Practice Perfect Posture: When I walk into a room, people immediately know that I am the one in charge. I don't have to tell them I'm in charge, they have already decided I am before I even open my mouth. I communicate this information to them primarily through posture.

Posture communicates our status within a group more than the clothes on our back and the words coming from our mouths. It only takes a second for someone to start making decisions about me. So I make sure to instantly communicate authority and power through the way I hold my body.

I stand and gesture using specific techniques that subtly show dominance and control without seeming like a tyrant or manipulative. These techniques include standing erect, using gestures with palms facing down, and with filling my space.

The brain is programmed to equate power with the amount of space they take up. Standing straight makes you look taller and holding the shoulders back maximizes the space I take up. But if I slouched, I appear project submission and weakness.

Maintaining good posture helps others understand that I am someone worth knowing. While using my space to make broad and expansive gestures shows others I know my limits. These combine to command respect and help others to value engaging with me.

Adopt a Likable Tone: Coming into an interaction defensively or acting like I want to fight is naturally off-putting. It sets me up to be rejected and makes the other person retract. If my intention is to influence a subject, I need them open and welcoming, not closed and defensive.

So I approach them as an old friend, helping them relax slightly and naturally open up. By showing I am comfortable, it signals to others that they should be as well. It's surprising how welcoming people can be when they relax a bit.

By acting friendly and open, they almost instinctively respond with warmth. They may remain suspicious of your intentions if you overplay it though. So be friendly, not fake, and believe that people want to help.

Example: When I meet someone for the first time, I smile and introduce myself in a familiar way and ask something about them. I begin my encounter on the basis that we are old friends meeting again. This helps me with the next trick...

Mirror Body Language: One of the most important elements of attraction is believing that the other person understands you on a deep level. The feeling of someone just getting you is intoxicating. The more we feel they understand us the deeper our connection.

It's important to emphasize commonalities rather than differences. The more we have in common, the more likely we are to align our motives and goals. These situations show us that the other person is similar to us. Since body language communicates the most information in the shortest time, it's the best way to establish that feeling of similarity.

People naturally mirror body language. We often don't think about our stance, tone, and position in conversation consciously. By monitoring and mirroring the other person's body language, it sets them up to be more attracted to me and value my opinion higher.

Example: Be subtle! If the other person shifts their weight to lean against a wall, lean up against it too. If they talk with their hands, I make sure to gesture when I talk. If they cross their legs, I do the same but in a slightly different position. I don't make huge changes, just enough to be in sync with the other person.

Establish Control: Once we are in sync, I begin to lead the conversation. I continually build rapport and when the time is right I begin changing my body language to encourage them to mirror me. Once they follow my lead, I know that I am in control and can diffuse an intense situation or build excitement.

The fastest way to gain trust is to mirror the other person's body language. Before I start leading, I have to get them to be in sync with me. The better I can do at mirroring and tone, the faster they sync up and I gain control of the conversation.

Questions help establish control of a conversation. It may seem counter-intuitive, but the person giving answers is weaker than the person asking the questions. So I ask questions as often as possible, although I rarely give the other person time to answer them.

Once in control, I can lead the conversation where I want. All the while I watch and study their reactions. I keep tailoring my questions and responses to encourage the other person to respond emotionally. The more emotion I can work up, the more control I have.

Example: If I want to convince a person to sign a contract, I control the conversation by asking questions and mirroring their body language. I'll cross my legs if they cross theirs and make similar gestures as my subject. Once their body language starts syncing up with mine, I ask questions like, "What are you going to do once you sign?" and "I can't believe we managed to get these terms. You must feel pretty lucky right?"

Make Eye Contact: We are the only primates in the world with white in our eyes. That's because we use them as a primary way to communicate. The eye is called the window to the soul because of how integral it is to body language.

Without good eye contact, people will perceive you as nervous, shifty, or unattractive. Making eye contact with someone creates an intense connection. That connection is integral to appearing trustworthy and engaged.

This doesn't mean to stare people down. Eyes can communicate aggression as easily as timidity. Refusing to break eye contact can make others uncomfortable and appear overly intense.

Example: I maintain eye contact for about 80% of my interactions. When the other person is talking, I maintain eye contact unless they are talking about something in eyesight or are becoming overly excited. I lower my eyes to communicate sadness, raise them for praise and keep my eyes mainly on the speaker.

Give Good Face: When talking about body language, we tend to focus on the torso and limbs. Things like posture, where and when to touch someone and how to hold our hands dominate the conversation. We often underestimate the power of emotive expressions.

It always surprises me how effective a smile is in communicating emotions. It can indicate pleasure, happiness, irony, appeasement, or a superiority complex. A genuine smile is one of the most underrated aspects of attraction.

We are the only primates that smile at people we like. The others see it as a threat display. People naturally find a mouth full of pearly white teeth to be very attractive.

Just make sure any smile you give is genuine. When people realize you are faking a smile, it sours their disposition. It gives away that you are deceiving them and calls everything you do and say into question.

Deception

Deception is a key aspect of dark psychology. Like many other dark psychological tactics, it can be difficult to tell whether any given instance of deception is dark or not. Before we explore the difference between dark and normal deception, let's first understand exactly what deception is.

A lot of people would state the viewpoint that lying and deception are the same thing. This is inaccurate. Lying is a form of deception but is by no means the only form deception can take. Rather than thinking of deception as "lies" it is better to think of it as "misleading." Any action or word capable of making someone believe something other than the truth can be accurately termed deception.

So what are some common manifestations of deception? Lying, omitting the truth, implying falsehood or fraudulently providing evidence for something false are all examples of deception. You will probably realize that you have done some of these things at some point yourself. Does that mean that all acts of deception are examples of dark psychology? Not at all.

Everyone deceives to some extent or another. People might deceive others for a range of reasons such as kindness, embarrassment or feelings of inadequacy. For example, studies have shown that many, even most men will lie about their height on dating websites. This does not make them practitioners of dark psychology! People even deceive themselves about a range of issues including their health, ambition, and happiness. Such regular, day-to-day examples of deception do not equate to dark deception. So what does?

Deception can be seen as dark when it is carried out with either a negative or indifferent intention toward the person being deceived. Normal deception is usually motivated by an inability to face up to the truth in one way or another. Dark deception, on the other hand, is an understanding that the truth does not serve the deceptive aims of the deceiver. Therefore, the truth is either changed, hidden, or ignored in favor of a version of events that better suits the purpose of the person deceiving.

Put simply, people who deploy dark psychology use deception to harm, not help. They help their own interests, but at any cost, regardless of who gets hurt.

Some people assume that if a deception is small scale it cannot be seen as dark, whereas larger deceptions must be inherently dark. This is not the case. By exploring the idea of the deception spectrum you will see that it is not the size of a deception that determines whether it is dark or not, rather the purpose behind the deception.

The Deception Spectrum

To understand the idea of deception it is important to understand that it can occur on either a large or a small scale. One of the main mistakes that people often make is assuming that deception is only serious if it is big and does not matter if it is small. This is a grave error. Small deceptions can be used in a powerfully dark way by skilled manipulators and are often more effective than large deceptions. Similarly, some of the largest deceptions ever carried out have been performed by deliberate manipulators to serve their own aims and objectives. Dark examples of various types of deception, large and small, will now be presented to illustrate the idea of the deception spectrum.

So what are some of the ways that smaller deceptions can be used by people who practice the art of dark psychology? Often, small deceptions are used initially to test the victim's gullibility and condition them into believing the deceptive statements and actions of the manipulator. If people are conditioned to believe a range of smaller lies over time, they are more likely to believe a larger lie in the future. This gradual conditioning is not the only way smaller deceptions can be used as a dark psychological weapon.

Smaller deceptions can also be carried out to undermine a victim's trust in their own powers of logic and reason. If a manipulator deceives a victim over small issues, and the victim begins to question what is happening, the victim may well conclude that their suspicion is irrational and they therefore cannot trust their own judgment. Most people are more likely to conclude that their own judgment is faulty, rather than another person is deceiving them over seemingly small issues. Users of dark psychology are aware of this general "trust" that people have and seek to exploit it without mercy.

Large-scale deception can also be an example of dark psychology in practice. One of the largest deceptions possible is to convince someone that you are a different person than you say you are. Not in terms of personality or some other detail. An entire identity. Name, date of birth, everything! The most skilled users of dark psychology are able to persuade other people to buy in entirely into their portrayal of a false identity and background.

Now that it has been shown how manipulative users of dark psychology are able to use the deception spectrum for their own aims, we will explore some of the most common topics and subjects that people are deceived about. We will then look at exactly how these large- and small-scale deceptions are carried out by exploring the specific tactics that are used.

Deceptive Topics

Everyone has heard the old saying that "money is the root of all evil." This is an exaggeration, but money is certainly the route of many deceptions. Deception and money can cross paths in many different ways. Some people deceive to attain money, others deceive to hide their own money, or lack thereof. Because money is such a common topic, some of its deceptive uses will now be explored.

One of the most common dark psychology deceptions involving money is carried out by the professional beggar. These are individuals that aim to extract money from the public despite having plenty of it. These beggars draw on a number of dark psychological principles to get money from innocent victims.

Such beggars have been known to inflict injuries upon their own body to appear more desperate to victims. Some of the most extreme deceivers in this area have even turned their own children into heroin addicts to use them as part of their scam. This is an example of the depths that money-related deception can sink to.

Marital status is another common area where people choose to deceive. Sometimes, people try and hide their married background to seduce a new victim. This can be for either financial or sexual or other reasons. Some people have multiple wives spread out across the world who do not know about each other. This type of deception has become harder with the advent of the Internet and the ability to check up on people via social media. The best deceivers are able to hide their tracks expertly and keep each fraudulent wife separate from the next.

Some people choose to appear falsely married when they are in fact not! This type of deception can occur for several reasons. A married couple is often perceived as more trustworthy than a couple that is not married. Some users of dark psychology are aware of this perception and use it for their own schemes and plans. Some people pretend to be married for reasons related to tax and insurance. One of the most common deceptions of this type is the creation of a fictional dead husband or wife to gain people's sympathy and, often, their money as a result.

A criminal background is another area of life many people are deceptive about. This is because it is almost impossible to be trusted professionally or personally if you have committed certain crimes. For example, if a man meets a woman, and the man has committed a serious crime in his past, how likely is he to tell the woman he has just met about this? It seems doubtful that he would be entirely upfront. Interestingly, such deception is not always dark. If the man does it through fear of being rejected, this is not dark deception. If he does it with the intention of hiding the truth to later harm his new victim, then this is a clear indication of dark psychology at work.

One of the most evil and deplorable examples of deception related to criminality is when someone who has committed serious past offences, such as rape, hides these in order to commit similar actions in the future. People with a dark psyche of this type are often compelled by their abnormal urges to the point they will do literally anything to hide the truth and carry on giving in to their compulsions.

Manipulators also feel that deception is a great way to hide any abnormal or socially unacceptable feelings they have. This stops their victim from being alerted to the kind of person they really are until it is too late. For example, if someone who uses dark psychology is interested in a person only for sex, they know this focus is likely to be a red flag to their victim and will therefore deceive their victim. They may either overtly lie or imply that their true intention is love and commitment. The victim falls for the deception, the manipulator's exploitation is complete and yet another person is hurt by deception.

One of the most common areas to be deceptive in is the truth of a manipulator's personal feelings for a victim. Deception is the most powerful tool the manipulator has to influence a victim to perceive things in the way the manipulator wishes, rather than how they really are. Typically, deception will be used in relation to interpersonal feelings to portray the manipulator as something they are not. Some of the most common examples of this use of deception will now be provided.

Within the field of romantic relationships, deception is often used to mask the manipulator's true intentions. Deceptive words and actions will leave a victim feeling as if the manipulator "just happens to be" what they are looking for at that particular time in their life. In actual fact, skilled manipulators are able to identify vulnerable people and probe their psychological needs and weak points. This information can then be used to deceptively cloak the manipulator and make them appear to be something they are not, but something the victim wishes they were. This deception is often the starting point of more complex, long-term manipulations.

Deception can also be used to soften up the victims' feelings in a non-romantic context and increase their susceptibility to manipulation. If, for example, a manipulator is looking for a vulnerable person to use dark psychology against, they may initially portray their own intentions as innocent. Even if the intention is to become intensely close to a person, the manipulator will usually deceptively portray himself as a very casual, easy-going person. This deception can be prolonged if needed. The manipulator will be whatever the victim needs, for as long as the victim needs, in order to get their guard down and allow the thorough manipulation to begin.

Deceptive Tactics

You now understand what exactly dark deception is, its spectrum and the common areas people are deceived about. Now it is time to examine closely the specific tactics used by manipulators to darkly deceive. Each of the tactics is equally powerful and careful manipulators know exactly how to use each at its most impactful and harmful time. It is important to note that manipulators will not neatly alternate between the four following categories—any given deception is likely to involve a blend of each.

Lying is perhaps the most obvious and common form of dark deception. It is likely to be chosen as a technique when the manipulator has decided that their victim is susceptible to lies and unable to gauge the truth. This may be because the victim is a generally trusting person or that the manipulator has carefully worked on their target over time to lower their guard. If a manipulator has chosen to deceive through the use of lies then it is likely they have also thought of a way to hide their lies and explain any discrepancies the victim may notice. Manipulators are masters of having a "plan b" at any given time during their dark deception.

Deception through lying is likely to occur in a subtle and thought out way. A skilled deceiver is likely to embed their lie into truthful information over time. For example, a manipulator will probably tell a story that is 90% true and 10% false. The victim will perceive the story as entirely true and not have any way of separating and ascertaining the truth regarding the deceptive 10%. Some manipulators also spend time associating truth with a particular tone of voice or gesture. They can then say something falsely deceptive in this tone of voice, or with this gesture, and it is likely to be perceived as true by their victim's subconscious.

Implying is a more subtle form of deception than out and out lying. Implying involves suggesting something false is true rather than boldly stating it is. Let's illustrate this idea with an example. If someone wanted to deceive a victim about the amount of money they have then they could either lie or imply. A lie would sound something like "Oh I'm a successful guy. I've made a lot of money," while the manipulator is well aware this is not the case. An implication may take the form of "it's so stressful trying to handle things with my accountant. Trying to get my tax bill down takes a lot of my time." The manipulator has acted and spoken in a way that implies they are wealthy without flatly stating it.

Manipulators often favor implications, such as those just mentioned, as they provide plausible deniability. If the victim accuses the manipulator of lying, the manipulator can say they did no such thing, and technically be truthful. Implications are also powerful if a victim happens to have an active imagination. The deceptive implication can be seen as a seed planted in the mind of the victim. The victim's own imagination then does the manipulator's work for them and fills in the blank spaces to create an idealized version of reality, according to the manipulator's prompts.

Omission is a failure to mention something that is true. This stands in contrast with other forms of deception such as lies or implications. Both lies and implications use falsehood to cover truth, to varying degrees. Omission instead goes the route of simply ignoring the truth and leading the victim's attention away from it. For example, if a manipulative user of dark psychology had an aspect of their past they did not want their victim to focus on, they would simply never mention it. They would draw attention to other times in their past or swerve the subject whenever possible.

One way omission is often carried out is by creating an "emotional fence" around a situation. This is a tactic in which a manipulator implies that a particular period of their life, or topic, is too painful or uncomfortable to discuss. The victim will then avoid talking about this time, or asking awkward questions, of their own volition. If the victim does bring up the subject the manipulator wishes to avoid then the manipulator can play the "it's too painful" card. This allows them to avoid the truth while making the victim feel guilty for touching on a "painful topic"!

Fraud is the most elaborate and criminal form of deception used by those who deploy dark psychology. Think of fraud as a lie on steroids. Instead of simply lying about something from their past, a fraudulent dark deceiver will have false documents, stories, and other evidence to back up their lie. The most skillful deceivers will use such things in a subtle way. Rather than saying, "no, I really am a Doctor, look at my certificate!" they are likely to make subtle displays such as leaving the fraudulent evidence around for their victims to see for themselves. Deceivers know that if they are too "pushy" with their fraudulent claims then the victim will intuit that something is wrong.

Worryingly, fraud is more common than ever thanks to the prevalence of computers and the Internet. Deceivers are able to use professional-grade software to quickly and easily make realistic-looking documents of almost any type. Such frauds can be carried out for either personal or professional reasons. Some of the most serious types of professional fraud include instances where people have obtained jobs using a false identity, stolen from a company, and then disappeared before their identity can ever be known. Personal frauds include terrifying tales such as people with HIV spreading the disease with the help of falsely produced certificates of clean sexual health.

When dark deception enters the realm of fraudulence it is a sign that the deceiver is a dangerous and committed user of dark psychology. For a person to risk running afoul of the law and facing serious criminal charges, they have to be truly committed to the manipulation they are attempting. If many users of dark deception are amateurs, the deceptive fraudsters are the dangerous professionals that must be avoided at all costs.

Ironically, one of the main ways dark deception is often carried out effectively is following the manipulator's own pantomime of feeling deceived by their victim! Many manipulators know that, by portraying their victim as the deceptive party, they are able to deflect any attention away from their own deceptive efforts. This is an example of a deception within a deception and shows the complex, layered approach to manipulation that many deceivers use.

Chapter 3: NLP

Neuro-linguistic programming (NLP) is an approach to communication, personal development, and psychotherapy created by Richard Bandler and John Grinder in California in the 1970s that leverages the power of language to influence thought.

NLP has infiltrated every element of modern business life. Everyone in sales or marketing has practiced these methods to some degree, but psychoanalysts and occult leaders around the world give it a bad name.

Most people don't grasp the underlying principles and struggle to apply them in everyday environments.

But some skilled individuals can harness this power to give them an unbeatable advantage. The techniques are best used in a one-on-one or small group environment. The fewer people involved, the easier it is to read and apply NLP methods.

NLP is a complex subject and is often taught over the course of years. That's because it takes practice to learn the range of reactions people can express. But the promise of learning people's inner secrets makes this technique especially attractive to con artists and law enforcement.

NLP is basically a method of reading a person to understand their personality and individual quirks. NLP users watch for subtle cues that are invisible to most people and use them to control a conversation and the emotions of the people in it. Eye movement, skin flush, pupil dilation, and nervous tics all provide information.

After an initial round of observation, skilled users can mimic their subject in subtle but impactful ways. The NLP user thus opens their target to suggestion and steers them toward an intended destination.

A skilled NLP user can determine:

Which side of the brain their subject uses

People fall along a spectrum between creative and analytical. New science shows that brain function is actually distributed across the brain. But it is still helpful to think of people through this lens.

Word choice, sentence structure, and associations all reveal details about the person that uses them. I begin by looking at what my target is saying and how they present their points, then I adjust my words to be more analytical or emotional based on my subject.

Left-brained people often use words that elicit emotion or experiences. Right-brained people like to include things outside their experience or expertise.

Example: Left-brained people: "That looks fun. I bet we can squeeze in!" Right-brained people: "Is that safe? Is it rated for someone my size?"

Which sense is most important to them

We have more than the five senses (sight, sound, taste, touch, and smell) most people know about. We also have a sense of order, balance, morality and a host of others, and each of us has one or two that are more important than the rest.

I listen to see which sense is most important to my target. Then I use some of the same words they did in my reply.

Example: If vision is important to my subject, I say things like, "Do you see what I'm saying?" Audio-focused people respond better to "Can you hear where I'm coming from?" Meanwhile, I might ask a taste-oriented individual to "savor that for a moment."

How their brain stores information.

Our brains are the most complex computers we have ever come across. They store and process billions of bits of information a second. Each one functions a little differently. One of the biggest areas of divergence is in how people store information.

Some individuals have a memory like a sponge, soaking up everything near them. Others are more like a strainer that catches big chunks and allows everything to pass through. NLP techniques help people discern the difference and to what degree.

Over time, NLP users get better at keeping track of information. With enough time, users can improve their information tracking abilities to near-genius levels. This gives us an advantage over anyone who isn't as experienced or naturally gifted.

I use this information to determine how much info I need to overwhelm my subject. If I want to lose them in the details, I simply include more than they can keep straight. If I want them to follow along, I keep the details and figures to a minimum.

Example: I will occasionally remember something wrong on purpose. It's best with something small like a phone number or address. If my subject corrects me, I can see how well they store information. The average person can only hold seven numbers in their head at once so it normally only takes me asking for them to remember two phone numbers to see where they fall along the spectrum.

When they are lying or making things up.

People perform specific behaviors when they make things up called "tells." NLP users like me can pick up on these tells and be able to call out the liar as they lie. Some people are better than others at lying but everyone has at least one tell.

Skilled liars understand that for someone else to believe their lie, so must they. So they convince themselves of it first. They often don't display all the signs of dishonesty because they truly believe the lie as they tell it.

Practice can help people fall for their own lie but the process demands a selective memory. This feature is more reliably detected than the oft-cited slight downward glance. It also proves to be a more consistent indicator of ingrained deception than awkward looks. Power imbalances also make a refusal to make eye contact less reliable as well.

Example: When my best friend (let's call him Ted) won't look me in the eye during his story. He keeps looking down and to one side of me, then the other. Another person (let's call him Fred) tells his story without looking away at all.

When Ted looks away I become suspicious, but Fred's refusal to look away is also a red flag. If they are subjects, I cut them some slack. As long as they don't change demeanor mid-story I can attribute some of it to simple nervousness.

How to make someone drop their guard.

NLP users like myself leverage these techniques to convince others that I am just like them. People can't help but like someone they recognize as a kindred spirit. So I combine the techniques above to highlight our similarities.

The more alike we are, the more a subject likes me. So I listen intently to what they are saying. Then I respond to them with the signals that I know appeal to their inner selves. This encourages my subjects to reveal more about themselves to me willingly.

When someone likes you, they want to include you in their lives. Listening to what they say often provides deep insight into what controls their lives. People offer up their darkest secrets willingly, believing that I truly understand them.

So you can condition people without their consent/knowledge.

Let's face it, people don't like finding out someone was manipulating them. It violates the idea that we are in control of our lives. But sometimes the truth is hard to take, and we need someone to help us see the way without calling us out on it.

We all manipulate those around us to one degree or another. This can be as simple as breaking a bad habit or establishing new relationship rules with a toxic family member. By steering them in the right direction, we can help them respond how we prefer.

NLP doesn't brainwash someone (that's covered elsewhere) or cause them to do something out of character. But it does reveal the strings that control each of us. What you do with those strings once you have them is up to you.

Once the subjects are open and receptive, I present my request in terms that they would prefer. I use strong action words with leaders, comforting and kind words with emotionally sensitive subjects, and common words with the less educated. I do everything in my power to appear similar to my subject in thought and deed. This ensures they are the most receptive to my desires and avoids having to issue orders and ultimatums.

Example: When I need a favor, I never ask for it right out the gate. Instead, I begin by building rapport. I ensure my body language is open and tailor my questions and responses to the person I am trying to influence.

Proponents of NLP believe that how you behave has a certain structure to it. Therefore, NLP aims to examine this structure to redefine the way your brain performs and responds to the information it receives. NLP helps you understand the things that make you tick. It opens your eyes to how you perceive the things that happen to you and around you on a daily basis. When you fully understand these things, you can handle situations in a better manner, and communicate more effectively.

Your neurological system is responsible for transmitting all the information your brain receives from your environment. In this context, your environment refers to everything external including all your organs- your ears, your eyes, your skin, stomach, lungs, and every other part of your body.

Your brain processes the information from all these parts of your body and transmits them to your brain and vice versa. For instance, once your brain receives information, it processes it and decides if it is good or bad news, and then transmits it to emotions that could be joy, tears, or laughter.

The takeaway here is that your brain determines how you respond to everything going on around you and how you communicate with others. Now, imagine being able to somehow, alter the way your brain handles this information and force it to react in a certain way. That is the whole logic behind NLP.

NLP helps to change your personal programming (think of computer programming: how programmers can change computer code to get a device or software to perform specific task or behave in a specific manner). It helps you re-organize your internal programming so you achieve the desired results you want.

To frame it in a simpler manner, NLP helps you achieve the following:

1. Increases Your Chances of Success: Generally, life is problematic and your day-to-day life whether at work, with your family or at leisure will be full of challenges. NLP helps you change how you view these challenges as well as your outlook on life. It helps you change the way you see life so that unimportant things stop weighing heavily on, or bothering you. It gives your life a deeper meaning and helps you organize your priorities.

It helps you identify your strengths and weaknesses so you can concentrate on things that can help you become better and more efficient, which helps you become more successful.

2. NLP Improves Your Communication Skills: NLP fosters positive thinking, which makes all your communications positive. It helps you redefine how you think and feel, which makes you a better verbal and non-verbal communicator, which then makes it easier to share your perspective with others and become.

So in essence, NLP helps you to become better at expressing yourself.

3. NLP Synchronizes Your Body and Feelings: When your mind and body are not in harmony, putting your thoughts and plans into action becomes very difficult. However, once you start using NLP, you unify your mind, body, and feelings so you can create a better connection and work towards achieving your goals.

You now have a better understanding of what NLP is and what it can do for you. Before we start using it to reprogram our behavior and maximize our potential, let us delve a bit deeper into its history:

NLP: A Brief History
John Grinder and Richard Bandler founded NLP in the 1970's at the University of Santa Cruz, California. At that time, Richard Bandler was a (AMIS) Information Sciences & Mathematics Master's level student while Dr. John Grinder was a professor of Linguistics.

They both studied people who they believed to be exceptional communicators and very good at helping their clients achieve desired results and necessary change. Particularly, they were interested in finding how it was possible for some people to effectively deal with difficult or sick people, defying the odds where other people have failed.

Grinder and Bandler chose to study three renowned psychotherapists- Virginia Satir, the developer of Conjoint Family Therapy, Fritz Perls, the founder of Gestalt psychology, and Milton Erickson, one of the major contributors to the development of Clinical Hypnotherapy. They also studied the skills of two linguists- Noam Chomsky and Alfred Korzybski, as well as social anthropologists Gregory Bateson and Psychotherapist Paul Watzlawick.

Neuro-Linguistic programming eventually exploded to include other disciplines and spread to several other countries. Unfortunately, in the 1980's, due to some dissatisfaction that Grinder had about some coding work they did together known as the 'classic code,' Blander and Grinder had a falling out. This led to a separation that led Grinder to team up with Judith Delozier to form newer models later named 'The New Code.'

Neuro-Linguistic Programming has come a very long way and many scholars have developed new codes, techniques, and versions, thus making it easier for ordinary folks to apply it in their lives to effect real transformation.

Although originally developed for use in the field of psychotherapy, professionals now apply NLP in all fields including Doctors, Accountants, Engineers, and every other profession in the world; from the way it looks, the future of NLP continues to look bright.

The Pillars Of Nlp: How To Apply The Knowledge In This Guide

To understand how to apply NLP to your personal life, you have to understand the four pillars of NLP. The four pillars of NLP are rapport, sensory awareness, outcome thinking, and behavioral flexibility.

1. Rapport: Rapport refers to how you build and maintain relationships with yourself and other people. Rapport teaches you how to say no to requests and things you do not want while still maintaining a good professional relationship and friendships with the people whose requests you reject.

2. Sensory Awareness: Another pillar of NLP is sensory awareness; sensory awareness teaches you how to pay closer attention to the things going on around you- how to make better use of the senses of sight, sound, touch, hearing, smelling, and taste.

3. Outcome Thinking: When you face a challenge, instead of being stuck, NLP teaches you to focus on what you want and helps you make decisions that will help you achieve these things.

4. Behavioral Flexibility: This refers to how you do things and handle situations. NLP helps you to do things differently. It gives you flexibility and the ability to change a course of action when one course of action leads to failure.

Authors Romilla Ready and Kate Burton describe how the four pillars can translate into your day-to-day life with this interesting illustration.

Imagine you ordered a new software to help you record all the names, addresses, phone numbers, and other important friends and clients' details. After spending time to purchase and install the software, you discover the software does not work because it has a coding bug.

You contact the software company's customer service department and they are rude and unhelpful. At this point, you have to employ your rapport building skills with the customer service manager so they can listen to your complaints. You would need to increase your sensory awareness by listening carefully, controlling your feelings, and deciding on the most suitable response. You have to know the outcome you desire by engaging in discussions with the customer service manager; do you want a refund or a replacement. Lastly, your behavior needs to be flexible enough to accept other outcomes if the desired one is unachievable.

That is how NLP helps you to become a better communicator and helps you achieve the things that you want without a lot of stress or frustration.

NLP Presuppositions

NLP presuppositions are basic generalizations or general beliefs in NLP that can be useful to you when you act as if they are true.

Some common presuppositions of NLP include:

1. The Map is not the Territory: Alfred Korzybski takes credit for this statement. He explains that we experience the world through the human senses of sight, touch, hearing, taste, and smell, which he refers to as 'the territory.' The experiences you get from these senses then transfer to the brain where they make an internal representation that he refers to as 'the map'.

You create an internal map in your brain; your experiences shape this map, but another person who has had the same experiences would never have the same exact internal map like yours (their perceptions and the way their senses perceive information may be different). This simply means that what is outside can never be the same as what is inside your brain.

If you are a doctor, what pills mean to you may be vastly different from what they mean to a patient and even a law enforcement agent. The point is that we all make different internal representations of the same things depending on our backgrounds and personal contexts.

To be a better communicator and a generally better person, you need to learn how to see things from other people's eyes- try to understand the internal representations or map of the person you are trying to communicate with. Rather than respond negatively to other people's behavior you may deem inappropriate, focus on trying to understand why that person might have behaved that way. This would make you a happier person who accepts people's actions and inactions with greater ease.

2. There is no failure, only feedback: This very important NLP presupposition will help you, but only if you can live by it. There is no one person in the world who does not experience setbacks and failures. It is up to you to choose whether to allow those setbacks to bring you down or you want to take lessons from your setbacks and these lessons as a learning experience that helps you become better at whatever you failed at the first time when you decide to try again.

Whenever you fail at anything, rather than give up, always ask yourself these five questions:

* "What am I trying to achieve?"

* "What have I been able to achieve so far?"

* "What are the things I have learned (feedback)?"

* "How can I use the lessons learned to better my performance?"

* "How am I going to measure my performance and success?"

3. The Meaning of the Communication is the Response it elicits: How the person you are communicating with perceives the information you are trying to pass across is the most important thing. No matter how good your intentions are, your listener interprets information based on how they receive it.

The onus therefore, rests upon you to pass your messages across carefully in the way you want your listener to receive it. Before you start communicating, have a clear understanding of the desired outcome of the conversation, and then carefully construct your conversation to elicit the exact response you want.

4: If What You Are Doing Is Not Working, Do Something Different: This is yet another presupposition and a very simple one at that. Do not be fixated on things that do not work for you, instead, change your tactics.

Determine why what you are doing is not working and what you can do to get better results.

5: You have all the Resources You Need to Create Desired Outcomes: Everyone has what it takes to develop, grow, and become a better version of themselves.

6: People are Much More Than Their Behavior: The fact that a person is behaving badly does not necessarily mean he or she is bad. People behave badly when they do not have the inner resources to behave differently. Most times, helping them change or improve on these resources would help them improve their behavior and start behaving better.

7: Body Language is Important: When communicating, you have to employ the right body language because body language makes up for 55% of how others receive your communication.

For the techniques to work for you, you have to practice them. Most of the techniques listed here are not instant solutions that are going to work in one day; however, with consistent practice, your life would improve and you would get better at what you want to improve.

1st NLP Technique: Setting Personal Anchors

Anchoring focuses on helping you change your state of mind. It can help you stay calm in the face of danger or trouble, and can help you relax and behave in a positive way when people are trying to provoke you.

Anchoring tries to mimic one of Pavlov's experiments. Pavlov experimented with dogs and sounded a bell as the dogs were feeding. Whenever the dogs saw the food and heard the bells, they salivated in anticipation of the meal. After some time, Pavlov began to sound the bell without the food in sight and he noticed that the dogs salivated whenever they heard the bells even without seeing the food.

Anchors are similar; they stimulate a response in your mind and help you control your thoughts and emotions. For instance, rubbing your forehead can be an anchor. Sometimes, anchors can be involuntary. For instance, a familiar smell might bring back a memory from your childhood or a song can trigger a memory of your ex. These are examples of involuntary anchors that work automatically without any self-induced trigger.

Establishing anchors involves producing stimuli when you experience the resourceful state so that the resourceful state pairs with the anchor. Just like with the dogs that begin salivating without a meal in sight simply because they heard a bell, you can establish personal anchors that will trigger a desired response in you whenever you experience anything.

Activating the anchor refers to the act of producing the anchor after you have established it in a bid to trigger the occurrence of the resourceful state.

When you are happy or sad, you are responding to some anchors in your life. When you are feeling motivated and confident or otherwise, you are also responding to some anchors although sometimes, you do not even know what these anchors are. That is why sometimes, you may be in a bad mood without knowing why.

The NLP anchoring technique teaches you how to design personal anchors and use them to produce a desired state of mind. For instance, if you are in an interview situation and you are feeling jittery, but you want to be calm, you can use established anchors to trigger a calm response within yourself. If someone is annoying you, but you do not want to lose your temper, you can use anchors to calm yourself down.

The Resource State

In the last section, we established that we all have the resources we need to achieve the things we desire. Here, the resource state refers to memories of the required state. For instance, if you want to be calm, your resource state here is a memory of a past time where you were calm and relaxed.

The resource state involves striving to make a previous experience vivid so it feels as if you are experiencing it afresh in the present. If you cannot recall a situation where you have felt that way, you can simply just imagine yourself in the resource state.

Types of NLP Anchors

There are three different types of anchors:

1. Visual Anchors: Visual anchors involve using the things you see to provoke a response. For instance, if you want to feel powerful, you can use your wristwatch as an anchor so that any time you want to feel powerful, you simply look at the wristwatch and use it as an anchor; however, the anchor does not have to be objects- you could use people, symbols, drawings, or anything physical as an anchor.

2. Auditory Anchors: Auditory anchors involve using sounds or music as anchors to provoke a response.

3. Kinesthetic Anchors: Touching yourself or imagining someone touching you is an example of a kinesthetic anchor.

How to Set Personal Anchors

To set anchors:

1. Decide the state you wish to anchor (the response you want to elicit e.g. Calmness, happiness, feeling powerful, feeling relaxed, etc.). It is helpful to write down your intention in your journal, so that you can crystalize exactly the feeling or emotion you wish to create a trigger for.

2. Choose the anchor you want to use to trigger that state. You can use a combination of anchors such as visual and auditory anchors.

3. Close your eyes.

4. Tap into your resource state by recalling a memory where you previously experienced the state you want to trigger.

5. As soon as you can vividly recall that experience, activate the anchor (play the music, touch the parts of your body you want to use as anchors, or look at the object you wish to use).

6. Release the anchors as soon as the experience starts to fade away. It is important to release the anchor immediately the experience begins to fade so that you do not anchor a drop in that state rather than the state in itself.

7. Take a break and do something else such as counting from one to ten.

8. Repeat the process from step 1; this time, make the memory more vivid and then try to establish the anchor at the highest point of the experience.

9. Test the anchor to see if the required state occurs. After you have solidified your process, be sure to record everything about your process, to make sure that it is repeatable. What emotions came up during this process? What memories did you specifically trigger? Did you use visual or auditory cues? Write down everything.

10. Check the anchor the next day and continuously until it becomes permanent.

You should always ensure the anchor fires in the same way every time you want to link to the resourceful experience. If you cannot get a desired state when you trigger the anchor, change the anchor to avoid establishing a negative anchor.

2nd NLP Technique: Pattern Interruption

Imagine a situation where you have a favorite route you drive through each time you are going from home to your place of work (every day). This driving pattern becomes repetitive and sometimes, you do not have to place too much effort and concentration into it because well, you already know the drill.

It is kind of like autopilot for you and you take out this time to think of the tasks you need to complete at home, how your day went, and other things while your subconscious takes care of everything else.

Suddenly, you hear a loud sound and bam! A large tree has just fallen and your path is obstructed. You slam the brakes and the car comes to a screeching halt. For the next few seconds, you are sitting in your car wondering what just happened.

Your subconscious is not used to this situation; therefore, it does not know how to respond. At this point, you have to step in; your conscious mind has to take control and issues instructions detailing how to handle the situation. Your subconscious mind is great at running automatic patterns so that your conscious mind can handle other activities that need conscious handling.

When you are trying to alter some patterns, sometimes, automatic habits, thoughts, emotions, and actions can create a problem. It is not as if you are not willing to change, but your subconscious keeps pulling you back, which then cause you to do the same thing repeatedly.

Well, you have to understand that the subconscious mind is very poor at decision-making. Only the conscious mind has the ability to make decisions. As an NLP technique, pattern interruption forces your subconscious mind into a state where it waits for information from your conscious mind.

It helps you break habits and embrace new methods and changes. It helps you re-program your subconscious so that the subconscious becomes a messenger that receives instructions from the conscious mind.

How to Practice the Pattern Interrupt Technique

To practice this NLP technique:

1. Decide on a particular behavior you wish to change. This has to be something you do automatically without thinking about it. For instance, eating junk food whenever you are watching TV could be an example of something you want to change. Write down in detail in your journal exactly what you would like to change.

2. Start observing how the pattern runs. At what point do you start to experience the urge to eat something? At what point do you decide to get up and walk to the fridge? How do you make a choice of what to eat from the different available choices? Record your decision making process in detail in your journal.

3. Create a pattern interrupt completely alien to the behavior you wish to change. For instance, when you experience the urge to eat something, fold some clothes or instead, drink some water. You need to create a pattern interrupt entirely different from the usual pattern. This pattern interrupt has to jolt you just like the tree that fell in front of your car. Again, write down in detail the new behavior you are going to implement.

4. Every time you feel the urge to engage in the pattern you wish to change, use your pattern interrupt to do something else.

Continue to impose this pattern interrupt and before you know it, you will eliminate the habit you want to change and the new habit will replace the old one (as such, the new habit has to be a positive one). You can use pattern interrupt to get rid of addictions and any negative behavior you wish to eliminate from your person. Reflect on the effectiveness of this technique and how it is influencing your behavior.

3rd NLP Technique: The Swish Technique

The Swish NLP technique helps you alter how your memories affect you. It helps you disconnect from powerful negative thoughts that provoke negative feelings that may negatively affect you and your life.

You can use the swish NLP technique to manage your thoughts

and feelings especially thoughts and feelings related to the things happening around you. This NLP technique helps you disconnect from past thoughts such as things that irritated you or made you feel embarrassed in the past, present feelings caused by self-undermining thoughts, and anxieties about forthcoming or future situations.

For instance, if due to illness or stress, you take a leave from work and you find yourself worrying about getting back to work, you have an unwanted negative feeling that in this case, is worry. Each time you remember you have to walk into your office when you resume work next week, your stomach churns and your heart starts racing. This means that walking into that office is the trigger.

You have checked this feeling to see if there are any rational reasons for your fear, but there are none because you have checked with your employers and everything is good. Now, you do not want to be worried and afraid whenever you think of walking into your office next week. You want to be confident and enthusiastic about it.

You can use the Swish technique to replace these feelings and change them into positive ones.

How to Use the Swish NLP Technique

To use the swish NLP technique:

1. Identify the feeling you want eliminate.

2. Identify the thoughts or images that provoke the negative feeling.

3. Check if your fears are founded and rational. If they are simply irrational, move on to the next step.

4. Close your eyes.

5. Create a replacement image in your head. This means you should identify how you want to start feeling. It means you should begin to see yourself acting the way you want.

Now, what you want to do is to point your thoughts towards a fresher and more positive direction. The idea is to re-program your brain by changing the trigger so you can know when you should start thinking new thoughts.

6. Think of the trigger image (the negative one) then start inserting the replacement image in between the trigger image. In between worrying, start imagining yourself feeling more confident. Before you begin, write down your replacement image in as much detail as you can, to help you solidify your visualization.

7. Allow the replacement image to become bigger and more vivid so that the trigger image begins a gradual disappearance.

8. Break the state and open your eyes.

9. Start from step 1 and this time, try to insert the replacement faster.

10. Repeat the process about 5-7 times.

11. Test it to see what happens when you try to recall the negative trigger image, you will discover that it becomes more difficult to bring back the negative feeling.

If, however, the negative trigger continues to manifest, the trigger may be more powerful than the Swish technique. In that case, try a stronger technique like the anchoring technique. Reflect on the results of the Swish technique in your journal.

4th NLP Technique: The NLP Framing Technique

The NLP Framing technique draws upon the idea that how you perceive everything depends on your point of view. Framing involves trying to change the meaning you attach to a thing by trying to change its context or setting.

For instance, a person trying to annoy you can seem funny so that, rather than becoming angry, you can start laughing at what the person is doing. The meaning you attach to events and things happening around you is dependent on how you frame it.

You can use your responses and behaviors to change the meaning. Dressing as a skeleton to a Halloween party and dressing the same way to a burial would cast different perceptions even though it is the same costume and the same person wearing it.

NLP reframing helps you change how you see and perceive things happening around you so you can behave in a different way. You can get people to see things differently by reframing events and communication differently to get a different response. By using this technique, you can keep calm in the face of fear and maintain your cool when you should be angry or losing your temper.

How to Use the NLP Framing Technique

To use this NLP technique:

1. First, identify a behavior you consider negative or troubling; a behavior or feeling you would like to eliminate from your persona.

2. Now try to establish a communication with the part creating the behavior or response. This could be a sensation in your body, a picture of another person, a specific sound, or voice: anything that triggers the negative behavior or feeling. Write down both the behavior and any triggers associated with it.

3. Ask yourself what exactly you want- what would you rather feel instead? How would you rather behave? You have to recognize the difference between the feeling/behavior and your intended one.

4. Tap into your creativity to figure out three alternative ways you would rather feel or behave instead of the current negative one or some alternative ways to get your intended outcome.

5. Evaluate your new choices and determine whether they are acceptable or not.

6. Check for objections with other parts. Sometimes, when you change an ingrained behavior or pattern, it affects other parts or aspects of your life. You have to ensure your new choices and desired change do not have unintended consequences.

The framing technique helps you tap into your inner resources so you can behave in a way than is far different and superior to your normal way of thinking. Write down any reflections and results from using this technique.

5th NLP Technique: Mirroring and Building Rapport

Mirroring involves mimicking or copying the behavior, body disposition, or speech patterns of a person you are communicating with.

Note: mirroring is very different from aping someone. Aping is where you copy everything someone does; that is not mirroring, that is rude.

Mirroring is subtle and barely noticeable by the person whose body language and speech patterns you are trying to mimic: it has to seem unconscious.

To Mirror someone, you can mimic his or her:

* Speech patterns

* Body language

* Vocabulary style or specific choices of words

* Pace, tempo, pitch, tone, and volume

Mirroring helps you create rapport with the person you are engaging in communication. It makes it possible for the person to warm up to you, trust you, and understand you. A successful interaction can only happen when you maintain rapport with the person you engage in communication with.

There are two approaches to mirroring: you can emphasize the similarities between you and the person, or you can emphasize the differences. Emphasizing the similarities eliminates resistance and antagonism.

Mirroring is a natural thing that most of us do. For instance, if you are trying to talk to a little child, you may crouch so you and the child can be at the same height, or you may talk slowly so the child hears you and understand you better. This is an example of how we naturally mirror others.

How to Practice the NLP Mirroring Technique

To practice mirroring:

1. Mirroring Body Postures: This involves adjusting some parts of your body (or all your body) to match the other person's body posture. Ensure that the posture is a natural one; otherwise, the mirroring may seem disrespectful. You can mirror a person's head and shoulder positions or other natural poses.

2. Mirroring Breathing Patterns: Another thing you can try to match is the breathing pattern. You can mimic the depth or rate of someone's breathing; however, if this breathing is irregular, you should not mimic someone's breathing pattern.

3. Mirroring Voices: You can try to match the voices of those you communicate with by matching the volume, pace, pitch, and choice of words. This can be a very tricky thing to do, but if you learn to do it subtly, you will be better for it because it will improve your rapport building skills. You do not have to mimic every aspect of a person's speech, but you can speak slowly if the person speaks slowly, or speak in a high tone if the person does so.

4. Mirroring Beliefs and Values: Another way to mimic someone is to try to understand his or her values and believes, and try to see that person's perspective. This is not real

mimicry because you do not have to agree with that person's believes and values; you just have to understand him or her and avoid levying judgment. Doing this helps build rapport and makes people more likely to warm up to you.

5. Mirror Language Patterns: You can also mirror a person's language patterns. Marketers and sales representatives commonly use this approach. It makes the person you are communicating with feel understood. What you have to do is to use the same words the person uses or use similar paraphrasing. This ensures the other party feels listened to and understood.

Essentially, mirroring makes the person you are communicating with feel as if you are on the same page. It makes the person feel heard and understood, which ensures the person feels comfortable and at home when conversing with you.

For the next few days, make a habit of mirroring and matching people when communicating. Write down your results and observations. Did it improve your communications? How so?

Chapter 4: Psychology Of Influence, Persuasion And Manipulation

Manipulation literally means using something as a tool to suit your own purposes. The act of manipulating others typically involves using other people as tools. You can't have remorse or shame if you want to be a successful manipulator. You need to view people as pawns that you move around the board game of life. People are very useful; why not use them?

Manipulation has a bad reputation. It's a dark art because it involves making people act against their will or without their knowledge. Nevertheless, this does not mean that manipulation is always used for bad. Sometimes you might use manipulation for positive purposes, such as causing people to make wise decisions. It can benefit the person that you are manipulating as well as yourself. Sometimes manipulation only benefits only you, but it does not harm the other person. You don't have to use manipulation to hurt others, though it is certainly useful in that respect. Manipulation is a valuable skill to possess because it really helps you gain the upper hand and get what you want. It enables you to use people to their full capacity to further your own goals and aspirations.

It is crucial to be sneaky when you manipulate others. People hate being manipulated and made to do things that they do not consent to. But keep in mind that most people have manipulative tendencies and manipulation is far from rare. Therefore, you are not a bad person for using the manipulation tactics included in this chapter. You are simply going after what you want. That makes you powerful and even positive. Just make sure to hide your manipulation attempts and disguise your intentions. Otherwise, people will judge you harshly and get mad at you. You can lose friends left and right if you gain the reputation of a manipulator. We talk more about hiding your manipulative tendencies and actions in Chapter 8 and Chapter 10, but we talk a little about this in this chapter too.

So let's delve into this fascinating and useful subject, shall we?

Make Someone Your Pawn

You can't just manipulate people with whom you don't share a rapport. You have to build a rapport and prime your subject before you can successfully manipulate him. This means that you need to form some sort of relationship with the person. Using a combination of psychological tricks, you can make a person weak for you. Your subject will be willing to do anything for you if you break down his mind and soften him to your attempts at manipulation.

Priming is best achieved through emotional manipulation. You want to play with someone's emotions. The first step is to make someone feel great around you. When someone likes you, he will be more open to your persuasive attempts and will want to please you. He will want to spend time around you because you make him feel good. This time enables you to get your hooks into his mind more successfully. So start with meaningful flattery. Observe your subject to see what means a lot to him. Then compliment him on the things that he values and cares about. For instance, if he loves sports and plays softball on the weekends, talk about sports with him and compliment his pitching techniques or his athletic physique. Over time, he will become increasingly attached to you.

Next, start the emotional roller coaster. As you get to know this person better and make him feel more and more attached to you, start to make him doubt his self-esteem. You can do this by finding things that he is guilty about, or making him feel guilty about things that he does. Always play the victim and make him feel like a terrible person. It's possible to pout like a child but it's even better to act like an adult and pretend to get very hurt about small things he does while telling him that you forgive him. You will look better if you pretend to be an adult who always takes the high road. He will become even more infatuated with you and may start to admire you.

Guilt is very powerful. But so is self-doubt. Plant seeds of doubt in his mind so that he feels insecure. Make him start to hate his friends and family by telling him about horrible things they do or say so that he doubts his social support network and his value to other people. Cause him to question his abilities and skills by saying things like, "You know that you're not good at that!" or "That's not one of your strengths." Tell him that you are simply opening his eyes to his inabilities so that you can protect him from the pain of failure or the pain of being around his hurtful loved ones. Then follow each little insult up with compliments. This will make him very confused. He will start to doubt himself and he will believe what you say because he is attached to you. People are quite sensitive to suggestion, so this method works incredibly well. Meanwhile, he still feels like you are a nice person who cares about him. He won't be ready to end all contact with you just because you insult him from time to time.

You also want to provide him with multiple rewards for what he does for you. When he pleases you, show it and lavish him with praise or favors. Also do favors for him and provide him with lots of services or support so that he is more open to doing favors for you. This is the basic principle of reciprocity, where people like to return kindness and favors that others do for them. You can use the things that you do for him as a bargaining tool. Call on him to return a favor sometime, and he will likely be willing to reciprocate. If he is not willing, guilt him by reminding him of a favor you did for him a while back.

The final part of priming is making someone doubt his sanity and perception. Tell him how he is wrong and come up with convincing arguments as to why. Inform him that he is making things up or misremembering things all of the time. Over time, this will chip away at his security and certainty in his own mind. This method is known as gaslighting, and it is one of the best ways that you can prime someone. Don't take gaslighting lightly. You can use it to totally drive someone crazy over time. It's actually a great form of psychological warfare against someone close to you.

Even if you care about someone, you can still prime him without hurting him. Make him dependent on you so that he never leaves your side. You don't have to be romantically linked to someone to accomplish this sort of dependency. Just offer him something that he can't get anywhere else. Make yourself very useful to him and bolster his ego so that he relies on you for his happiness, convenience, or even financial stability. Disable his other forms of support so that you become the only person in his life. You don't necessarily need to use gaslighting, guilt trips, and other such methods to hurt him; being nice is enough to gain a foothold on someone for persuasive methods. As a friend, lover, or even co-worker, you can accomplish this priming at varying levels. You can do it lightly to someone whom you want to manipulate only slightly. Or you can do it very heavily to someone whom you want to use for life.

Get a Good Read on Someone

There is another side to priming that you really need to take into account. This side is reading. To manipulate someone, you must get a good read on someone. Natural manipulators are adept at reading people at a glance. If you are not so good at reading people right off the bat, then you can use time and priming to get a good read on your subject.

Basically, you want to get to know the person very well. Listen to everything he tells you and glean his speech for potential emotional weapons to use against him. Anything he confides in you or accidentally reveals to you can be turned into a weapon at any time. Save these weapons in your back pocket for when you need to use them.

What are the best emotional weapons? Guilt is probably the most powerful one of all. People hate feeling guilty. So find out things that he feels guilty about.

Also find out things that he loves or cherishes. You can give him these things to make him happy and reward him for his work for you. Or you can cripple him by destroying these things. Love and passion give people power and a will to live. Taking these things away can crush a person. Try to become the gatekeeper of the things that he loves so that you can gain ultimate power over him. For example, bar his access to his loved ones and pitch a fit when he talks to people that you don't approve of, but let him talk to the people he loves whenever he does what you want.

Another way to use what someone loves against him is to trivialize things that he cares about. If he says how much he loves a dish, tell him how it is really not that good. Ruin the small things that he loves. Then you can move on to bigger things. Also, trivialize his opinions. All people love and value their own opinions and believe that they are right. If you make him feel stupid for having certain opinions, then you will be able to chip down his self-esteem and make him doubt his rightness. Make him feel small by trivializing him in every way possible. Eventually, he will come around to your way of thinking and will love only the things that you love because you have made him abandon all that he loves. You will make him feel small and stupid so he will look to you for validation and approval in order to repair his damaged ego.

Trust is a great weapon that you can use. Most people desire to be trusted. You can tell him that he is not trustworthy because of various things that he has admitted to. Then make him do what you want for the sake of winning your trust. Let's say you're dating a guy and you want to manipulate him. Tell him that you don't trust him because he admitted to cheating on his ex. Tell him that you worry he will cheat on you. Or claim that you have been cheated on, so now you have trust issues. This way, he will want to win your trust. He will jump through hoops to make you trust him, including cutting off people you don't like in his life. You can make him cut off female friends and friends who encourage him to drink and have a good time without you around by saying that you feel threatened by these people.

You can also use his reputation to manipulate him. He wants to be liked by others, so you can use that as a weapon. Tell him, "If you do that, everyone at work will hate you. You don't want that, right?" Most likely, if he's a normal person, he will agree that he wants people to like him so he will reconsider doing anything that might damage his reputation. Encourage him to do things by saying that it will gain him favor with different key people. One great way to manipulate co-workers is to give them "tips" on how to please the boss and possibly earn raises or promotions.

Insecurities are fantastic weapons. Whatever hurts him will become apparent rather quickly as you get to know him. Some people are so obvious about their insecurities that you will be able to read what they hate about themselves right away. When someone becomes quiet after a certain subject is brought up, you can bet that he feels insecure about that subject. You can also guess what bothers him based on blatant flaws that he has, such as excessive weight or a poor relationship with his wife. But mainly, you will learn his insecurities by listening to him. Listen to what he talks about and notice the things that seem to bother him or that he complains about. These insecurities are things that you can bring up at opportune moments to hurt him. You can also urge him to do things to atone for what he lacks, or to fix a flaw that he perceives in himself. In addition, you can plant new insecurities in his mind by casually mentioning flaws that you notice in him or saying nasty things to him about himself during arguments.

Finally, his level of affection or even love for you is a powerful weapon. This is why friends or lovers will say things like, "If you really love me, you won't do this." This is also why people like to threaten to leave. You can threaten to withdraw your love from him to goad him into action.

Play the Victim

Playing the victim is your number one "get out of jail free" card in life. If you become adept at playing the victim, you can pretty much justify anything that you do and make your subject feel terrible about anything that he does.

First of all, you want to believe that you are the victim. You can accomplish this by rationalizing things. Use your conscious processes to justify your actions. Think of ways that others have wronged you in order to excuse your actions. As long as you believe that you are the victim, then you won't feel guilty about playing the victim card.

You also want to establish your innocence and vulnerability. You want to appear like an innocent victim being harmed by life so that others feel sorry for you. Tell people sob stories about how the world is against you. Make sure that your situations are not self-imposed so that others don't get irritated and think that you just blame others for your own problems. A good example of this is talking about how you were abused as a child so that you can explain why you have difficulties picking good love partners and healthy friends now. This excuses your actions and makes you seem like a victim who cannot control your own mind or help yourself. Strike sympathy in others so that people want to support you.

When your subject does anything that you don't like, play the victim card. Show him how deeply he has hurt you. You won't accomplish this by pouting, giving him the silent treatment, or throwing a wild tantrum. You will enjoy way more success playing the victim card if you appear mature and calm about something. Inform him in a steady voice that he has hurt you. Offer him consequences for his actions that he won't like. Say that you feel the need to protect your heart and your interests from him. Also, make him feel like a monster by continuing to appear like a saint who never does any wrong. You don't want to do something wrong to him that he can use as a weapon against you when you play the victim card.

Let's revisit cheating in a romantic partnership. If you want to prevent him from cheating, you can play the victim card when he talks to or looks at other women. But be very cautious that you never do anything with another person that makes you look bad. If you do cheat, make sure that he never, ever even suspects you of what you did. Never let him access texts or social media posts that he can use against you, or your whole victim plan will fall apart.

You can also very effectively play the victim card by telling other people what he does to you. Act as if you aren't complaining about him. Just casually mention things that he does that are abhorrent. Blow what he did out of proportion to make him seem terrible, but don't make it obvious that you are trying to complain about him. Instead, make it seem like you are the victim of his actions and you don't realize that you have been terribly wronged. Other people will become shocked and even outraged that he would do this to poor little innocent you. They may even become your soldiers, confronting him and making him feel guilty.

Guilt is your best trump card. Use it well. But also use it wisely. Playing the victim card too often will wear out its power.

Dr. Cialdini's Six Principles of Influence

You can use the Six Principles of Influence to influence any person to do what you want. These six principles are the foundation blocks of persuasion and manipulation. Keep them in mind and use them to gain influence over others. You can get what you want by using these principles.

The first principle is the reciprocity that we already discussed. Basically, you want to make people feel as if they owe you. Do favors for people so that you can call on them later when you need something. Appear very warm and generous so that others want to do things for you.

The second principle involves social proof. You basically want to be well-liked. The more popular you are, the more influence you have. Other people will back you up if you are well-liked. And new people that you meet will want to do things for you to gain your favor, since everyone else likes you.

Commitment and consistency is the third principle. People tend to stick to things that they know. They like consistency. So you can appeal to someone by asking him to do something that he already does. This works well in sales – if you have a customer who always likes the same types of products, you should target him with similar products. Brand loyalty is built upon this principle.

Authority grants you a lot of influence. If you appear like an authority figure, others will do what you say. The infamous Milton Prison Experiment is a classic example of how people are willing to obey authority figures to great lengths. Appear like you know what you are doing and be bossy. People will believe that you have more power than you really do if you act like it.

Scarcity is where you can essentially scare someone into action. Let your subject know that something is in limited supply. He will jump into action to get it before it runs out. This is the principle at play when TV commercials command you to act fast before supplies run out.

Liking is the final principle. This is where you want to make people like you. Being a kind, sincere person (at least on the outside) can make others want to do things for you. Also, appearing warm will make people like you. Approach someone with a proposal or favor in a warm room or offer him a warm drink to give the impression that you are warm. Use light touch, such as an arm brushing during conversation, and lots of eye contact to establish a bond. In Eastern cultures and some Native American cultures, eye contact and touch is not encouraged, so instead you want to appear deferent and deeply respectful at all times, keep your hands to yourself, and avoid eye contact.

Denial

Denial is extremely powerful. People don't want to believe things that hurt them. So they put up fronts and convince themselves that reality is just peachy. You can use denial to your favor when you are manipulating someone.

One way to use denial is to justify your own behavior to yourself. You won't be a great manipulator if you feel bad about what you're doing. You need to justify what you are doing to yourself. Denying the level of depravity that you have sunk to is a great way to do this.

Another thing that you can use denial for is manipulating your subject. Use his own sense of denial against him. Tell him that he is in denial about things to convince him that he is in the wrong. Make him think that you know him better than he knows himself. That will make him rely on you yet more for affirmation and validation of himself. It will also make him start to doubt himself and wonder what it is that he is in denial about.

Finally, denial is great for defending yourself. Vehemently deny any and all wrongdoing. Should someone accuse you of being less than upfront and trying to manipulate others, deny it. Never admit to any wrongdoing. You want to appear like you have done nothing wrong. This will make your subject believe it. If you stand steadfastly beside your innocence, you will appear more innocent. Eventually, your subject may cave and rethink his accusations. He may even stop suspecting you of any wrongdoing. Use this opportunity to convince him that he is just seeing things or being too sensitive or thinking of a past friend, lover, or family member who was manipulative to him. Tell him that he is projecting stuff onto you and that it isn't fair to you. Again, you want to whip out that victim card and even convince yourself that you are a victim. This makes the denial even more complete.

Chapter 5: Brainwash and Hypnotism

Hypnotism Is Real

Of all the aspects of dark psychology presented in this book, hypnotism is the one most likely to raise eyebrows. When most people hear the word "hypnotism" they think of a guy with a moustache and a top hat waving a pocket watch while insisting someone is "getting very sleepy." Believing in this stereotype is actually dangerous. This is because real hypnotists are out there and are equipped with subtle but powerful techniques. These people are able to draw upon the darkest elements of psychology to influence people in an incredibly powerful way.

So if hypnotism isn't the old stereotypical image of a stage hypnotist, what exactly is hypnosis? Simply put, it is the ability to make suggestions to someone that filter through deep layers of their consciousness. This ability to make deep, impactful suggestions to someone while they are in a vulnerable and suggestible state grants hypnotic dark manipulators a high level of power over their victims. Unlike almost every other technique in this book, hypnotism is not something that people encounter in a milder, more innocent form in their day-to-day lives.

Hypnotism can take the form of both verbal and nonverbal suggestive practices. Often, the forms of suggestion are very subtle and therefore difficult to detect. By its very nature, hypnosis works on the deepest levels of a person's mind. Someone who is skilled in generating a hypnotic state and response in someone will be able to bypass their defenses and influence them without raising any alarms or giving a person a chance to raise their guard.

Hypnotic Tactics

Now that you understand the difference between the stereotype of what hypnosis is, and what it actually is, it is time to explore the main hypnotic tactics. There are many variations on these types of tactics but they offer an insight into the main things to be wary of. Examples of how each tactic can be used will be provided wherever possible to give a clear insight into how hypnotists operate in our midst, undetected, every day.

Suggestion Can Be Silent

If hypnotism, in a darkly psychological sense of the word, can be understood as "deep suggestion," then it is important to understand what exactly is meant by suggestion in this instance. Most people might imagine a suggestion is a clearly stated statement like "I suggest you do this." This is far from the truth. The dark psychology view of suggestion is very far apart from the usual understanding of the word. The first important concept to grasp is the fact that hypnotic suggestion can be either verbal or nonverbal.

Picture the human brain as an iceberg. The part of the iceberg that is above the surface of the water represents the known and understood aspects of cognitive function such as thought. The larger, deeper part of the ice submerged below the water represents parts of the brain that are consciously inaccessible and little understood. If you doubt the power of this hidden portion of the brain you need only think of dreaming and the immense power of the mind to generate series of images, pictures, and sounds while a person is asleep. Dark hypnotists target their efforts toward this hidden, subconscious part of the mind.

There are, broadly speaking, two types of suggestion used by hypnotists—silent and verbal. Both types of hypnotic technique come in a variety of different forms. The exact type of hypnotism a manipulative person chooses to use at any given time depends on a range of factors. Some manipulators will carry out whichever form of hypnotism they feel will be most impactful on their victim's particular psyche. Others carry out whichever technique they happen to wish to use for their own amusement at the time. This depends largely on whether the hypnotist is seeking to exert influence in the most powerful way possible or is merely trying to control someone for their own fun and games.

Verbal suggestion is very difficult to detect. Sometimes, dark hypnotists are able to implant suggestions into their victim's mind using words that sound similar to other, more innocent words.

To take a deeply dark example, if a hypnotist was trying to instill suicidal feelings in their target, they may mask the true command of "You want to die" as something similar sounding such as "You want to dine." The hypnotist would speak the words "you want to die" clearly, but in a context that would mask the true content. For example, the hypnotist could talk about an upcoming trip and state "You have to check out the local restaurants, you want to die, somewhere that is popular but picturesque." The victim's mind would absorb the suggestion of death without consciously understanding why!

The above example of masked verbal suggestions is akin to a poison being hidden in someone's food. The victim consumes the hidden content, thinking that they are enjoying something helpful and innocuous when in actual fact they are absorbing something deadly. The especially devastating part of this technique is the fact the victim will never notice it. Even if someone thought they had picked up on the true words the hypnotist had spoken, imagine how crazy they would sound calling them out! People will generally take whichever option is psychologically easier for them and will therefore accept the masked command without question.

A hypnotist's tone of voice and choice of words is another method of verbal suggestion. Some hypnotists will carefully learn the pace and style of delivery a particular victim uses when they are expressing something serious.

For example, if, when someone wishes to say something meaningful, their voice lowers in pitch and slows in pace, the hypnotist would memorize this detail and retain it for future use. The hypnotist would then make suggestions to the victim in that exact, mirrored tone of voice. Because of the carefully modulated tone, the words delivered in that vocal variation would deeply penetrate a victim's defenses. Because the hypnotist would only deliver the suggestive content in that tone of voice, and then switch back to their usual way of speaking, the victim would be unaware even of what had taken place.

Another form of personalized, verbal suggestion employed by a hypnotic user of dark psychology is to pick up on words that have a special, intense significance for the victim who uses them. For example, when someone is very emotional they will often use a particular term to convey this feeling. If the hypnotic manipulator is able to pick up on these personal words then they are able to deploy them for their own benefit. Just as people have a specific tone of voice, they have a list of personal words of meaning, without often knowing it. The manipulator will understand their victim better than the victim understands herself. Knowing these words and tones, the manipulator can reverse engineer the victim's own brain to use against them.

Suggestion can also take nonverbal forms as well. This can be through the hypnotic manipulator's body language or even cues they place in their environment. If you think such seemingly trivial things could not exert a hypnotic influence then think again! Even political leaders have made use of such tactics in ways such as changing their hairstyle to convey a different intention during speeches. As discomforting as it is to believe, the human mind is deeply susceptible to even the smallest hints and cues.

So what are some of the main ways a hypnotic manipulator can use nonverbal suggestion against their victim? The technique centers around the idea of association. A skilled hypnotist is able to consistently link a strong emotion to some kind of external stimulus such as a particular eye movement they use. For example, if a hypnotist wanted to be able to trigger a feeling of panic in a victim, they may choose to make a particular motion with their eyes whenever the victim was thinking about, or experiencing, panic. The victim's subconscious would then learn to link the eye movement to the feeling. Over time, the hypnotist would be able to trigger the emotional response simply by making the eye movement, even without the need for any other stimulus.

Environmental stimulus is another form of nonverbal suggestion that forms a part of the hypnotist's toolkit. Think of environmental stimulus as like being summoned to the principal's office as a child. The location itself was enough to send you into a feeling of deep panic because you had learned to associate the location with panic and problems. Hypnotists are able to use this same concept to devastating effect in adult life.

For example, they will often be sure to have a certain type of conversation with a victim in one location only. Picture a hypnotist and their victim in a romantic relationship. Every time the hypnotist wishes to get some kind of agreement or consent from his victim, he may be sure to ask her only when they are at a certain coffee shop. Over a period of time, the victim's mind begins to associate the physical environment of the coffee shop with the granting of permission. The hypnotist can then use this physical environment as external psychological leverage whenever he needs to exert influence and control.

Vulnerable Victims

Hypnotism is not equally effective on everybody it is tried on. Some people are more likely to be influenced by a hypnotist than others. Although the exact level of susceptibility is complex and hard to simplify in a single sentence, it boils down to the idea of vulnerability. Vulnerable people are more likely to be agreeable to hypnotic suggestion than people who are less vulnerable. The types of vulnerability sought out by hypnotists in their victims will now be explored along with a guide to how hypnotists exacerbate and magnify the vulnerable paradigm.

The people most vulnerable to hypnotism are those who have recently experienced a significant life-changing event that has reduced their stability and certainty. For example, if a person has just come out of a serious romantic relationship, has suffered bereavement or lost their job, they are particularly vulnerable to suggestion. This is because the human brain craves certainty and understanding above all else. If a hypnotist spots someone who is in a vulnerable place they can offer them certainty and change their vulnerability in general to vulnerability around the hypnotist specifically.

There are roughly two facets of vulnerability in a hypnotist's victim—preexisting vulnerability and exacerbated vulnerability. The most diabolical hypnotists are able to combine both aspects to lethal effect. Not only will the best hypnotic manipulators be able to find someone who is suitably vulnerable, they will find someone who is specifically vulnerable to the hypnotic psychological scheme they have planned.

For example, if a hypnotist is looking to use their powers to gain financially, they might seek out a victim such as a rich, recently bereaved widow. They will then, subtly and over time, associate their own self with feelings of security and comfort while increasing the widow's general feelings of loss and vulnerability. Eventually, the hypnotist is the victim's only refuge from a hell of their own making.

As well as seeking out vulnerability in general, hypnotists are known to seek out situational vulnerability as well. This is when someone is in a situational circumstance that makes them more suggestible than their overall "baseline" of suggestibility. There are tactical tricks a hypnotist can use to ascertain this situational vulnerability. One such tactic is trying to induce "mirroring" behavior in their target. When people feel a subconscious level of connection and rapport with someone they will start to "mirror" the person without knowing they are doing it. To check this, a hypnotist might make some small change to their body language, such as a hand motion. If the victim subconsciously mimics this gesture, then it is a sign the victim is situationally vulnerable.

Now that both general and situational vulnerability have been explored, it is important to understand how the most skilled hypnotists use the two types of vulnerability together for an especially strong impact. If someone is vulnerable in general, due to their life situation, and vulnerable in particular, due to the situation the hypnotist has managed to set up, then that person is in the most influenceable state imaginable. Once such a state has been induced the hypnotist is likely to move on to the most powerful and advanced techniques they possess, such as NLP.

NLP

NLP, or neurolinguistic programming, is a technique that is powerful even in the hands of the most well-intentioned people. Leaders within the world of business and philanthropy are some of the most common advocates of the techniques and principles offered by NLP. Placing such techniques in the hands of people willing to use dark psychology to exploit others is like giving a nuclear weapon to a psychopath. They possess both the power and the will to create serious psychological havoc among their victims. Understanding the main techniques used by practitioners of dark psychology offers insight into the way they can be deployed to devastating impact.

Anchoring

Anchoring is an NLP technique that involves linking an emotional state to some form of external stimulus. If you are familiar with the idea of Pavlovian conditioning, then you will understand this tactic. Hypnotists are able to induce a powerful emotion in a victim and then link it to a stimulus such as a physical gesture or tone of voice. The hypnotist is then able to induce this emotional state at will by performing the linked stimulus.

The most nefarious hypnotists will use the principle of anchoring in a very subtle and underhand way. They will work for a prolonged period of time to induce a variety of different anchors in the psyche of their victim without the victim's conscious awareness of what is taking place. This provides the manipulator with a set of hypnotic puppet strings that they can pull as and when they desire. Often, hypnotists will use an "anchor stack" to induce different intense feelings in quick succession. For example, they will induce the feeling of love, followed by terror, followed by love once more, all in quick succession. This series of emotions overloads the victim's emotional circuitry and leaves them as mere clay in the hands of their controller.

Reframing

Reframing is the art of controlling the way ambiguous information is perceived. There is an old saying that "nothing is good or bad unless we believe it to be." Reframing is the ultimate technique related to this idea. Hypnotists can use reframing to effectively control the way their victim thinks and feels. Think of a skilled reframer as an editor. They are able to selectively choose the victim's focus and the feelings the focus triggers. This is effectively hypnotic mind control.

So how does darkly psychological reframing work in practice? Let's take a situation where a hypnotic manipulator has influenced a victim to no longer spend time around, or communicating with, a particular person. The victim may state feelings of sadness or loss related to this interpersonal change. The hypnotist would be able to reframe these feelings into ones which suited the hypnotist's own purposes. This is best illustrated through an example dialogue.

Victim - "It sucks I haven't spoken to Rachel as much, I miss her."

Hypnotist - "I know you might hate how things are with Rachel, but I know you're smart enough to love the freedom you have now."

Notice how the concept of hate is linked to Rachel and love is linked to the "freedom" of being without her? The hypnotist also plays on the victim's ego by linking the idea of their intelligence to going along with the way the hypnotist wants them to perceive the "frame," or perception, of the facts. Think about what you have already learned about the vulnerability of victims and you will understand how this reframing can be used to devastating impact.

Future Pacing

Future pacing is the closest thing possible to psychologically manipulative time travel. Future pacing allows a skilled manipulator to lead their victim on a mental journey into the future and influence behaviors and responses that will occur in the actual, chronological future that exists independent of the victim's reality.

At its most fundamental, future pacing involves the mental leading of a victim through a future scenario. For example, if the hypnotist wants their victim to feel generous and relaxed whenever they receive money, the hypnotist would ask their victim to envision a situation, such as receiving their next paycheck. To make this future imagining possible the hypnotist would ensure the victim imagined all of their five senses in action—what they would see, feel, touch etc. at the time. This helps the brain to perceive the future scenario as "real" due to its sensory depth.

Once the hypnotist cognitively transports their victim into the future, they begin to suggest certain happenings and monitor the responses. For example, the hypnotist may say something like "Imagine being very generous with this paycheck and providing it to those who really need it, because you are a kind person and doing the right thing is deep in your nature." If the victim's physical response to this future scenario showed signs of compliance and acceptance then the hypnotic manipulator would have the confidence that their victim would actually behave in this way when the scenario occurs in the future.

Due to the intensity and power of the hypnotic techniques mentioned in this chapter, the best manipulators only use them in moderation. For example, a darkly psychological hypnotist would be sure to keep their interaction with a victim 95% normal. This will increase the victim's comfort and trust to such high levels that the 5% time spent on hypnotic influence would not only slip past a victim's defenses unnoticed but would work to great effect once embedded in the victim's mind.

Brainwashing

Are You Brainwashed About Brainwashing?

If you ask someone if they know what brainwashing is, they

will probably reply that they do. Brainwashing is a concept that many people have heard of, while mistaking their vague familiarity for accurate understanding. Before looking at how, where, and why brainwashing occurs, it is essential to understand exactly what brainwashing is and isn't. Of all the dark psychology techniques contained in this book, brainwashing has the most serious and widest impact. If the other dark psychology techniques are sniper bullets, aimed at one particular person, brainwashing is a nuclear bomb capable of devastating an entire city.

The term brainwashing refers to the slow process of replacing a person's ideas about identity and belief with new ideas that are intended to suit the purpose of the person doing the brainwashing. Brainwashing can occur in both wider and narrower contexts. For example, a brainwasher is able to control one person in particular, or use the same techniques and principles to control the minds of a wider group at once. Brainwashing is the process that turns atheists into suicide bombers and prisoners of war into communists. It has been tried, tested, and proven over the years to be effective in almost any scenario.

So what are the most common misunderstandings related to brainwashing? Many people picture the process as some kind of quick and forced occurrence. Picture either Alex in "A Clockwork Orange" or Neo in "The Matrix" having concepts forced into their cranium, involuntarily, in a short space of time. This is Hollywood brainwashing and is far from what actually occurs in real life.

The process of real-world brainwashing will be explored in detail later in this chapter, but at its simplest, brainwashing is a process involving the slow, gradual, and seemingly voluntary changing of a person's "map of reality" from the one they have freely put together to one that is forced upon them by the brainwasher. The evil irony of the technique is the brainwasher will ensure the victim feels in control at all times.

Brainwashing Contexts

So what are some of the main situations that are fertile breeding grounds for brainwashers? Before the process of brainwashing itself is explored fully, let's take a look at the situations in which people are often brainwashed and the motivations behind this.

A lot of people would agree with the idea that "cults brainwash people" but few would be able to explain exactly what a cult is and how they brainwash their recruits. Let's demystify the process. A cult is a fringe group, often built around a charismatic leader who is able to exert high levels of influence over their followers. The cult will usually provide a "complete understanding of reality" to those who follow it. Why exactly is this cult context one in which brainwashing flourishes?

The primary attraction of cults is they present reality as something very simple and within reach of the average person, provided the person is willing to take on board the cult's teachings. We live in a complex modern world where life can seem confusing and overwhelming. Cults cut through this confusion and tell people "don't worry, we have the answer." The way in which this "answer" is presented is intended to play on the human need for belonging and acceptance. Brainwashing can flourish in this context as a result of the idea of the "new normal."

What exactly is "the new normal"? It is a way in which cults are able to influence those they brainwash into accepting their teachings by making them seem prevalent, accepted and positive. For example, the idea of worshipping a man who claims to be God would be incredibly strange in everyday life. Within the closed environment of a cult, however, this behavior becomes "normal" to the extent that not doing it would seem strange to people within the cult! This process of persistent, social reinforcement is one of the most powerful ways in which the ideological brainwashing of cults is able to occur.

Think of cults as drug dealers. Perhaps the newcomer to the cult had been seeking something in their life and came across the cult, just as newcomers to the world of drugs often, misguidedly, seek out their first high of their own volition. The cult doesn't need to "push" the drug of their ideology onto the victim as the victim was already seeking the fulfillment of a void in their life. It is this initial "search" and "readiness" on the part of the people who are later brainwashed that makes them so susceptible to the brainwashing process itself.

Ideologies are another context, similar to cults, in which brainwashing is commonplace. The difference between a cult and an ideology is the focus of the ideology is on the idea itself rather than the person delivering the message and those who follow them. Whereas cults brainwash people into placing faith and trust in the cult leader and their followers, ideological brainwashing involves leading people to place absolute trust in an idea.

Ideological brainwashing is incredibly dangerous due to the fact it goes above and beyond any one individual. Think of extremist religious terrorism, for example. It is possible for a high profile figure within the ideology, such as Osama Bin Laden, to be killed. Does this kill support for the idea itself?

No! The dead figures are praised as martyrs who gave their life to the ideology, thus increasing its attractiveness and allure to potential newcomers.

Almost any ideology is likely to have an extremist, fringe outskirt in which brainwashing takes place. Even something seemingly innocent like a pop band can have this impact. Young fans, at a psychologically impressionable age, link their sense of identity, happiness, and belonging to a pop group. They will gladly defend this group to extents that are unusually intense. Some pop groups have fans that even self-harm, using razor blades, if a member quits the group! If you carefully consider this phenomenon of the power of brainwashing even in accidental, innocent contexts, then consider how devastating the process can be in intended contexts like cults and terrorist groups.

Now that you have a clear understanding of the way brainwashing can occur in broader social contexts, such as cults and ideologies, it is important to understand that a personal, one-on-one context is also a ripe situation for elements of brainwashing to occur in. There are similarities and differences between "group" and "individual" brainwashing and understanding these nuances can help to identify when either type is occurring.

Personal brainwashing is similar to group brainwashing as it involves the slow and steady replacement of existing beliefs with new beliefs that serve the objectives of the brainwasher. Instead of relying on group dynamics to reinforce "the new normal," a one on one brainwashing situation will instead rely on a deep, personal connection between the brainwasher and the victim. This can be even more powerful than group brainwashing as the content can be modified and altered to the particular psychological constitution of the victim.

The Process Of Brainwashing

Now that you understand the reality of what brainwashing is, and where it occurs, let's take a look at the specific process itself. Distinctions will be drawn between the way in which the process applies to both group and individual situations.

The starting point of any episode of brainwashing is the mental state and social circumstance of the victim. This is the foundation upon which the rest of the process is entirely reliant. Brainwashing is not something that can be carried out on absolutely anyone. It requires the identification of a person who is seeking something or trying to fill a void in their life.

So what kind of people are ideal victims for brainwashers? People who have had their existing reality shaken up by a recent event are prime targets for brainwashers. For example, many of the Western men who have travelled to become terrorists in Syria, and detonate suicide bombs, have done so after the death of a close friend or relative. When their existing world loses its meaning and certainty, brainwashers can step in and provide that certainty in the form of a murderous ideology.

Once a brainwashing victim has been identified, either in person or via the Internet, the actual process of brainwashing begins. Contrary to the popular image of a brainwasher as a wide-eyed psychopath who will incessantly and angrily indoctrinate their victim, real-world brainwashers are anything but this. They will come across as calm, friendly, rational people who have their lives together in a way the victim does not. Imagine being homeless and being befriended by a celebrity. This is how the process of meeting their brainwasher for the first time feels for a victim.

The brainwasher will often work initially on creating a level of trust and rapport between themselves and their victim. This usually involves creating both deep and superficial similarities. For example, superficial similarities may involve surface level preferences like an enjoyment of the same sport or even food! Deeper level rapport may involve some "deep" shared experience in the past of both the brainwasher and the victim. Brainwashers will convincingly fake these if needed. If the victim shares the fact that they have lost a relative in the past, guess what? The brainwasher suddenly has a similar story to tell.

The false emotional warmth and connection explained above is not the only aspect of brainwashing that occurs initially. The brainwasher will often provide gifts and other favors to their victim. For example, the brainwasher may treat them to meals or send them gadgets or other useful items. This creates a sense of gratitude and indebtedness from the victim to their brainwasher and softens up any resistance the victim may initially experience.

One of the most powerful examples of the above initial kindness can be taken from Prisoner of War camps. When American troops have been captured in the past, their captors often offer them American cigarettes and speak to them in a respectful way. This reverses the expectations of the victim and opens the victim's mind to the further brainwashing process that is to follow.

A utopian presentation is the next step in the brainwashing process, following the initial victim identification and rapport building stages. This involves the brainwasher slowly and increasingly offering a solution to all of the problems that the victim has opened up about. This is always done in a casual, offhand way at first to avoid any negative experiences of pressure the victim may experience otherwise. This utopian solution is always whatever cult, ideology or personality the brainwasher is trying to convert their victim to—terrorism, communism or just a charismatic brainwasher's own need for validation and praise.

When performed correctly, the initial stages of this process will leave a victim craving more and more information and understanding of the solution that is being hinted at. The brainwasher may even withhold this information initially, as if it is something that the victim must work at being worthy of attaining. This will lead to a strong motivation on behalf of the victim to seek out and accept the information they are eventually provided with. Thanks to the preceding steps, the poisonous ideas that are being implanted into the victim will seem as natural and refreshing as cold water on a hot day.

Once the victim is being spoon fed snippets of their new belief system, and responding well to them, the brainwasher will be very careful to reveal the right things at the right time. This is a concept that is sometimes known as "milk before meat" or "gradual revelation." It basically involves the presentation of easy to accept ideas before anything controversial is revealed. For example, in the case of religious terrorism, recruiters may initially focus on convincing their victim that God loves them. This is usually quite acceptable. More objectionable ideas, such as God wants you to blow yourself up, are saved until far further down the line. At this point, the brainwashing has reached the point of no return.

You may be questioning way a victim continues to engage with their brainwasher once the objectionable ideas begin to become apparent. The reason is threefold. First, the already vulnerable victim now feels a strong sense of liking and approval of their brainwasher.

Second, the victim has invested time and sometimes money into the process thus far. This is known as the "sunk cost fallacy." The victim is loath to "throw away all their hard work" by walking away from the process.

Finally, the brainwasher is likely to have amassed a lot of secretive and sensitive information on their victim. This "dirt" can then be held over the victim's head, either discreetly or overtly.

Both the ideas of a vulnerable victim and the "sunk cost fallacy" make logical sense. The idea of blackmail and control may be harder to understand at first. Why would a victim respond well to such threats? Well, they are rarely presented in a threatening way. For example, if the victim has divulged a lot of sensitive information to a brainwasher, and then begins to give signs of walking away, the brainwasher may appear concerned and insist that "if I can't help you anymore with your problems, I need to make sure someone else can. Perhaps your family or boss need to know what's been going on with you, so they can look out for you when I'm not there."

Because of the deep sense of rapport and warmth the brainwasher has manipulated their victim into feeling, the above form of blackmail and control is often actually perceived as kind, compassionate behavior. It is often enough to make the victim see "sense" and agree to remain on the brainwashing path they have embarked upon. Brainwashers are adept at making the pain and struggle of walking away seem epic, so staying becomes the preferable, easy option by default.

The end product of this process is the victim believing everything they have been indoctrinated to view as the truth. The power of the process is that the victim will feel they have chosen these views as their own and have sought them out through their own volition. This leaves a previously normal individual as an indoctrinated psychological slave to something they have no idea even exists.

The Impact Of Brainwashing

The above analysis of the brainwashing process shows the severity and depth of the technique. It is inevitable that a process as powerful as this has lasting consequences. Some of the main impacts of brainwashing after the process has been completed will now be explored.

Loss of identity is one of the most serious side effects of brainwashing. A feature of many cults and ideologies is that people who complete their initiation process are given a new name. This allows the person's psyche to totally detach from their old identity. They can believe things and do things they would never have done before as the person they used to be no longer exists. When carried out carefully the brainwashing process leaves a victim feeling as if their old identity was no more real or permanent than a nightmare from which they have awoken.

So is brainwashing simply a process of ideas? Not at all. If brainwashing resulted in only the change of opinions then it would be far less of a problem than it actually is. The main danger of brainwashing is it not only changes the ways that people think and feel but also the way they behave. People go from functional members of the society with acceptable, positive jobs and interests to brainwashed zombies willing to carry out rape, murder, and suicide. This sounds sensational and dramatic, but it's true. Read on for the proof.

If you have any doubts about what brainwashing can drive a person to, consider the following examples. Members of some religious cults will gladly cut off all contact from their family, leave their careers behind, surrender all their wealth and possessions, and place their autonomy entirely in the hands of the organization that has brainwashed them. This is not all. The victim will see their new lifestyle as a blessing they are fortunate to have, rather than something unpleasant they have been forced into.

Another example of the toxic outcome of brainwashing is the repeated tale of young people becoming brainwashed by religious extremists to travel to a foreign land and drive a car packed full of explosives into a group of people they have never met and who have never hurt them. Such young victims are often educated people with a track record of success in life and a family history free of turmoil or abuse. These tragic losses of life are testament to the overwhelming, all-conquering power of the brainwashing process.

PTSD (post traumatic stress disorder) is another hallmark of those who manage to escape, or are rescued from, a situation of intense brainwashing. Brainwashing victims often show the same physical and psychological signs as war veterans who have witnessed their friends being blown apart next to them during combat. The severity of this traumatic aftermath shows that a brainwashing situation can harm a person as much as a world war.

Perhaps the most shocking examples of the long-term impact

of brainwashing are the numerous instances of people who have been rescued or escaped from a brainwashing situation, only to later return of their own free will. Even once they are outside of the controlling, brainwashing environment, the legacy of the process runs so deep through a person's mind, they seek to return to it. This is a form of Stockholm syndrome. The escapees will actually praise their brainwashers far into the future and defend, support, and justify the ideological stances they were indoctrinated with while captive.

Conclusion

Time to take a deep breath and assimilate all the information presented to you, in this book.

If you are experiencing a stressful time, it can be useful to learn relaxation techniques. They will help you manage your mental wellbeing. Many of these can be done in the privacy of your own home, or even in a work situation.

Your mental wellbeing is as important as your physical health. It plays an important role in your happiness. You owe it to yourself to break out of any unhealthy stronghold that others might place on you, such as a manipulative character. No one could be happy living or working alongside another person who belittles them. Most particularly if that person coerces them into doing something they don't want to do. That is exactly what living with a controlling person is like, at work or home. You will feel trapped as they slowly destroy your self-esteem. If your partner or work colleague is never open to compromise, then they may well be manipulative and controlling. A healthy relationship, be it personal or work related, should be one whereby everyone feels comfortable.

Most of us grow up to be taught the social rules of good manners and acceptable behavior. Unfortunately, some either ignore this learning process or have no one to teach and guide them. We need positive role models in our informative years. Those who may have suffered abuse either physically or mentally as children, will be scarred in some form or another. Many will still manage a normal life, but it's unlikely that anyone can come out of a bad childhood unscathed.

Many of us struggle on in our daily lives. We perform routine tasks to make our lives pleasant and our loved ones happy. There comes a time when we do not always have the energy or inclination to help other people. Most of us will do a kindness along the way. Always though, our priorities are for our own loved ones. There is a certain necessity to be strong if you wish to make something of your life. Otherwise, depression can set in and you may drown in the many temptations around you. Excessive eating, or even worse the temptations of alcohol and drugs could seem an easy way out.

It does take courage to stand up to a controlling manipulative character, but you must be brave and see it through. Push them away from your life and keep them at arm's length. Don't be taken in by their false promises. If someone encompasses you so tightly that you feel you cannot breathe, then you must escape. A healthy relationship should not feel like that.

This book should enlighten you on how to cope with some of the problems you may face in life. It is meant only as a guide on how to deal with controlling manipulative relationships. It cannot give you your freedom. Only courage can do that. Build up your self-confidence. Take care of your health. For the sake of living a happy life, learn how to handle such controlling characters that may pass you by.

Lastly, if you enjoyed this book I ask that you please take the time to review it on Audible.com. Your honest feedback would be greatly appreciated.

Thank you.

Now, I would like to share with you a free sneak peek to another one of my books that I think you will really enjoy. The book is called "Emotional intelligence 2.0: A Practical Guide for Beginners" Published by Travis Goleman and Daniel Greaves. It's A Practical Guide that will teach you to master Social Intelligence, Emotional Awareness and Relationship Management. You will also learn How to use Conversational Skills to Persuade and Influence People.

Enjoy!

Introduction

You have heard so much about emotional intelligence that your interest is piqued. Whether you are a top-management official at work or a stay-at-home mom, emotional intelligence is important in your life. I commend you for taking the steps to develop your emotional intelligence skills. By doing so, you will only improve your quality of life from how you feel about yourself to how you feel about others, and ultimately, how others feel about you.

I can do all that just by reading this book, you may ask? Yup! You sure can.

The following chapters will discuss how you can develop your ability to master emotional intelligence and to see great improvements in your personal and professional life. The book is divided into 6 easy-to-read chapters that will give you insight into how to manage your emotional intelligence.

The first chapter will give a brief overview of what emotional intelligence is. Then the subsequent chapters will break down the tenets of emotional intelligence into more detail. Chapter 2 builds on Chapter 1 and explores what emotional intelligence looks like in your everyday life. From this chapter, we dive right into building skills that will help you improve your emotional intelligence. In Chapter 3, how to manage your emotions will be discussed, followed by how to improve your self-awareness in Chapter 4. Chapter 5 explains how to use social awareness and relationship management respectively.

At the end of every chapter, there will be a special section dedicated to giving you skills on how to develop each skill in order to become better at emotional intelligence. Also, please note that throughout the chapters, you will learn about Valerie who does not have an idea about emotional intelligence and her socially bankrupt life reflects it. Please do not be like Valerie!

Hopefully, by the end of this book, you will learn a lot from Valerie on what to do and what not to do in regards to emotional intelligence. At the end of the chapter, bullet points of the chapter topics and activities you can do to help develop your emotional intelligence will be given. Take small baby steps and do not be afraid to feel awkward as you try to implement the changes associated with emotional intelligence into your life. Every journey must start with one step and it is difficult before it gets easier. By the time you finish, you will notice how much your life has improved just because you decided to take the step to be more emotionally intelligent.

Chapter 1: What is Emotional Intelligence?

Meet Valerie. Valerie is a typical American who is married with two kids, a house, and a white picket fence. Oh yeah, she has a beautiful black Labrador as well. Valerie would consider her to have an average level of emotional intelligence. She does ok at work. Her familial, personal, and professional relationships are so-so. She feels like she's walking through life. Not going fast or slow, but just regular shmegular. She doesn't always feel in control and sometimes has panic attacks because she is overwhelmed, stressed, and unhealthy. She figures everyone else is going through the same things so it is not a big problem.

Cut to one busy day where Valerie is rushing to work because she has not communicated to her family members that she needs help and all of the chores and housework falls on her. Not too mention, she had to stay late at work the night before because she is a people pleaser which made her oversleep in the first place. Picture Valerie in a car, speeding down the highway in the rain before she hydroplanes smack dab into an eighteen-wheeler. Her car spins out of control and Valerie finds herself pinned behind her steering wheel in her car that is sideways in a ditch. Of course, a Good Samaritan saw the incident and immediately called emergency services who rushed to the scene. After the paramedics help her out the car, she is whisked to the hospital.

The good news is, she was alive. The bad news is, she has amnesia and she has to learn everything all over again. Facts like her children's names, her husband's name, and her dog's name will be seemingly easy to learn. However, the nuances of emotional intelligence seemed much more difficult to learn. She has to learn how to identify her personal emotions, manage them when reacting to other people, as well as managing her social settings and relationships. Whew! Valerie is on a quest to relearn what emotional intelligence is, but Valerie is not alone. There are a lot of people who want to learn how to be emotionally intelligent and are on the same path as Valerie.

This book attempts to help people like Valerie and the readers navigate the tricky, topsy-turvy, abstract world of emotions and the unspoken rules that come with it. Unlike Valerie who is starting with a blank slate, most people have some type of experience with their emotions whether they have anger issues, are people pleasers, or are narcissists. Emotional intelligence draws upon your personal preferences and experiences to figure out how to survive in the world. In order to improve upon one's emotional intelligence, one must first understand what emotional intelligence is.

So what is emotional intelligence? Known in short as EI, emotional intelligence is the multi-faceted capacity of being in tune with your personal thoughts and emotions and being able to manage them in your daily living and in your dealings with other people. In order to be emotionally intelligent, you must first have mastery of who you are and know how to handle your emotions. Then you must know how to navigate relationships with other people, especially how to interpret and understand their emotions and how to be savvy in the way you respond to their emotions for optimal results. In other words, to be emotionally intelligent, you need to know what to say, when to say it, and how to say it. Sounds like a lot? You're right. Becoming emotionally intelligent can be overwhelming, but it is not impossible. It is a skill that can be learned with practice. Being emotionally intelligent is a trait many want to acquire because research has shown that emotionally intelligent people are deemed better leaders, better friends, and better family members. People with emotional intelligence do not necessarily have the highest IQ, but they understand how people work. As a result, their acumen in dealing with people helps them to be successful in a way that people who are not emotionally intelligent are not able to achieve.

Emotional intelligence was brought to the mainstream in 1995 by Daniel Goleman when he wrote the book *Emotional Intelligence: Why It Can Matter More Than IQ*. This book was seminal in changing how people thought about the power of emotions. Before this book, emotions were not seen as powerful tools to help you succeed. Emotions were seen as a hindrance. Goldman brought the importance of being emotionally intelligent to the forefront, but it was not an idea that originated with him. Way back in the day, over 2,000 years ago, Plato wrote that "All learning has an emotional base." Even though Plato had said that emotions were important centuries earlier, scientists did not always see it that way. However, in the 1920s, the idea that emotions were important re-emerged when Edward Thorndike named the ability to get along with others as "social intelligence."

In 1950, Abraham Maslow sparked the human potential movement and wrote about the importance of people enhancing their mental, physical, emotional, and spiritual strengths. From his research, lots of similar movements were launched and people began to build on his ideas. From this birth of new knowledge, two researchers, Peter Salovey and John "Jack" Mayer in the 1990s, have been credited with first using the term 'emotional intelligence.' In the article, Salovey and Mayer defined emotional intelligence as scientifically testable "intelligence." This work set the foundation for Daniel Goleman's book in 1995. From there, many different offshoots of emotional intelligence were developed. For the purpose of this book, we will focus on emotional intelligence as being composed of four different parts consisting of self-management, self-awareness, social awareness, and relationship management.

Self-awareness is being in tune with your emotions. If you are self-aware, you are great at identifying and deciphering your emotions and using them effectively when you react to a situation. Self-management is the act of managing your emotions and the reactions to any situation you may find yourself in. The word 'manage' is key in the definition of self-management. If you are great at self-management, it does not mean that you do not get angry or experience emotions at all. It means that you are adept at how you manage those emotions to get the outcome you want. Social awareness is being keen to the social environment around you. And relationship management is all about handling your relationships whether they be professional, personal, or even the relationship with yourself. In later chapters, each separate component will be delved into in greater detail.

To understand how one learns about emotional intelligence, a person must understand how our brains work. Our brain is divided into three separate parts — the basal ganglia, limbic system, and neocortex. The basal ganglia are at the root of our brain and it is considered the place where all our instincts reside. When you feel something in your gut, the information travels directly to this region of your brain without going through the other regions. This is information that you do not have to think about at all. The next part of the brain is the limbic system. The information processed by this part of your brain is considered to be processed on the subconscious level. Subconscious level information is a step above unconscious information and that information is right below our level of awareness. The subconscious level is where our emotions reside. It stores information about experiences good and bad that affect our behaviors, as well as it stores our value judgments. The neocortex is the next part of the brain. It controls your level of awareness. The information in this part of the brain is able to be accessed at will. It controls our reasoning, language, and thoughts. This brief overview of the brain is helpful to understand because certain activities suggested later on in the book target certain aspects of the brain. It is a cool tidbit to understand how the activities strengthen certain aspects of your brain so you can learn how to control your emotional intelligence better and be more aware.

Emotionally Intelligent Character Traits

How does someone who is emotionally intelligent act? People who are emotionally intelligent normally have a few characteristics that let others know they are emotionally intelligent individuals.

- Emotionally intelligent people have empathy. They are able to understand how others are feeling in any given situation. In other words, like the cliché says, emotionally intelligent people are able to walk in someone else's shoes. They are able to understand how someone with a sick child may be having a rough time or understand the importance of being nice to everyone whether they have experienced that situation or not.
- Emotional intelligent people also think deeply about their emotions and other people's emotions – a lot. They are pros at knowing how to relate and manipulate to other people in order to get the best outcome possible.

- Emotionally intelligent people do not run from criticism. They are able to take feedback easily without being defensive. They are able to take what people say about them, dissect the criticism, and take from the criticism what they may.
- Emotionally intelligent people are also genuine people. They seek authenticity in their relationships with other people and tend to see the best in people. Hence, they also are able to forgive and forget slights against them rather easily.
- People who are emotionally intelligent are very positive. They are not angels. However, they are effective at refocusing their thoughts, so they do not act impulsively and do something that they will regret later.
- Emotionally intelligent people do not run from confrontation. They face the criticism head-on and then go from there. They handle the conflict with ease, even if their egos are wounded in the process.
- Emotionally intelligent people are excellent communicators. They know their personality type and communication style and are able to effectively communicate with others and know the style in which they prefer to be communicated.

People who are not emotionally intelligent tend to be the exact opposite.

- They are easily flustered and easily angered.
- They are selfish and they only care about one person - themselves.
- They do not think before they speak and they talk all the time without any care to how other people may react to what they are saying.

- People who are not emotionally intelligent are usually not the easiest people to get along with.

Emotionally intelligent people are leagues ahead of people who are not emotionally intelligent. Interestingly, one can have characteristics of being emotionally intelligent and also have characteristics of not being emotionally intelligent. The key is to try and work on your emotional intelligence until you are competent in all four areas of being emotionally intelligent. This takes work.

For someone who has never ever thought about learning more about emotional intelligence, the information explained thus far may seem suspect. You may be one of the people who believe that emotional intelligence is a fluke. You may think that it is not necessary or important to be in tune with your emotions or in tune with the emotions of others in order to be a better person. You may think emotional intelligence is nothing but hippy-dippy foolery that has no place in the same sentence with rational thought. You may think that emotional intelligence has no effect on your success. However, think of that one person that you would not rather be around. This person always makes inappropriate jokes. They never know what to say. It is like they always have a foot in their mouth. These types of people have no self-awareness. No one wants to be around them. This is why emotional intelligence matters. There is no black-and-white version of emotional intelligence.

It is possible that you are good with some of the aspects of emotional intelligence and you need help controlling the other aspects. Perhaps you are good at knowing your feelings and you're able to manage your emotions, but you are terrible at communicating with others. Hence, your relationship management needs work. Perhaps you are excellent at navigating relations and social settings, whether they are professional or personal because you are great at putting on a front but your personal life is in shambles. You may need to work on your self-awareness. Or perhaps, you can easily be wonderful at managing other people's relationships. You can be the one friend that everyone comes to when they need help, but you are horrible at your own self-management. It happens. Just because you are okay with three out of the four aspects of emotional intelligence does not mean that you cannot improve the other aspects. Wanting to be aware of how emotional intelligence works is commendable and there are definitely skills and exercises that you can do to improve each and every aspect of your emotional intelligence core.

Yet, emotional intelligence can have a dark side. There are some people who are master manipulators. They are so good at emotional intelligence that they can draw upon what someone else is feeling in order to get the outcome that they want. These people know how to pit people against each other, play the victim, and play on people's emotions to remain in control at all times. If you are not emotionally intelligent, you can really fall victim to their traps rather quickly. One of the most important reasons for developing your emotional intelligence is to be a better person and to protect yourself against people who have nefarious intentions.

Lucky for Valerie, she is starting with a blank slate when learning how to develop her emotional intelligence. She does not have to be concerned about all the baggage that comes with learning a new skill. For her, she has to begin by learning what emotional intelligence is. So buckle up. The next chapter will go into more detail about how emotional intelligence affects our daily life whether we are aware of it or not.

Chapter Highlights

- Emotional intelligence was coined by Daniel Goleman in 1995 by his book *Emotional Intelligence: Why It Is More Important Than Your IQ*.
- Emotional Intelligence is composed of four different parts — self-management, self-awareness, social awareness, and relationship management.
- Our brain is composed of three regions that control our thoughts and emotions. By doing exercises to improve every aspect of our brain, one can improve their emotional intelligence.

Do the Work

- Why are you interested in learning more about emotional intelligence? Is it to improve personally or is it to improve in a professional setting or is it another reason? Knowing why you want to learn about emotional intelligence can help you when you get to a difficult spot in your learning.
- Do you think that you have more traits of being emotionally intelligent or more traits of not being emotionally intelligent?
- Emotional intelligence is composed of four different components — self-awareness, self-management, social awareness, and relationship management. Which component do you think you need to work on?
- Before emotional intelligence was brought to the forefront, there was a philosopher who said that "emotions are at the base of every decision?" Who was it?

Thank you, this preview is now over.

I hope you enjoyed this preview of my book Emotional intelligence 2.0: A Practical Guide for Beginners by Travis Goleman, and Daniel Greaves.

Please make sure to check out the full book on Amazon.com

Thank you.

www.ingramcontent.com/pod-product-compliance
Lightning Source LLC
Chambersburg PA
CBHW020122130526

44591CB00032B/339